The demonstrators stood in shocked silence outside the Atlanta jail as the police led him into the street.

MARTIN LUTHER KING WAS IN MANACLES.

The manacles reached down to his legs, dangling so that he stumbled when his guards led him into the police van. He raised his hand to signal to the demonstrators that he was all right, but there was fear in his heart. In the back of the van, behind a thin partition, was a huge German police dog that snarled and lunged at him when the guard slammed the door behind him.

"Where are you taking me?" he asked.

The guards did not answer, nor did they speak to him again during the ride through the dark night.

It was a night King never forgot. It was a ride filled with all the fears a black man could have in 1959. They could take you into the country-side and make you jump from a bridge the way they had Emmet Till not long ago . . .

When the van finally arrived at Riedsville Jail and the guards flung him into a solitary cell, King wept with relief and fear—and humiliation.

KING

**By William Johnston
Based on the screenplay
written by Abby Mann**

WARNER BOOKS

A Warner Communications Company

ISBN 0-446-89524-5

Warner Books, Inc., 75 Rockefeller Plaza, New York, N.Y. 10019

 A Warner Communications Company

Printed in the United States of America

Not associated with Warner Press, Inc. of Anderson, Indiana

First Printing: February, 1978

10 9 8 7 6 5 4 3 2 1

KING

1

March, 1968

An army of a sort was on the move along a downtown street in Memphis, Tennessee. The marchers were black men, their uniforms the patched and ill-fitting clothing of the poor. It was a most unmilitary army; no drums beat cadence, no attempt was made to keep the marchers in ranks. Their banners were hand-lettered protest signs that said simply: *I Am A Man.* They carried no rifles, no side arms. Their weapons were their unity—the fact that they had put aside individual differences to march together—and their newly-found belief that they were equal in worth to all other men.

At the eye of this storm of protesters, the black sanitation workers of Memphis, was Martin Luther King, Jr.—minister, civil rights leader, winner of the Nobel Peace Prize, perhaps the most celebrated black man in the United States.

There was little about King's manner or appearance, however, to suggest the classic leader. He was fairly small, given to roundness. His jaw did not jut; his eyes did not flash. On the contrary, his expression was wary and wondering; he seemed uncertain. Still only thirty-nine years old, in what would prove to be the last week of his life, he looked like an old fighter who relied on savvy to carry him through the battles, one who now found himself in the ring with a young opponent whose style was difficult to figure out.

Yet King was clearly the leader here. This was attested to, if in no other way, by the circle of disciples around him, most of them co-founders, along with King, of the black civil rights organization, the Southern Christian Leadership Conference. There was Ralph Abernathy, stocky, grim-faced now, but normally quick to smile. There was Andy Young, the cool one, the brilliant one, whose startlingly clear eyes, while focusing straight ahead, took in everything that was happening all around him. There was Larry McKeecham, bearded, burly —a dynamic, stomping man. And there was Bernard Lee, slim and wiry, combination friend, companion, and self-appointed watchdog for King. These men, special themselves, were, in the way they formed a protective wall around King, walking advertisements of his extra-specialness.

The march proceeded as usual, but through an atmosphere that tonight seemed alien, charged. What puzzled and disturbed King were the looks on the faces of some of the blacks who stood on the sidewalks along the line of march. He had not expected unanimous approval; wherever he had marched there had always been some black brothers and sisters who, out of the fear of change, had resented his determination to better their lives. In the past, however, those who feared had been the middle-aged and elderly. Tonight the dissatisfied faces were young, and the look in their eyes was not fear of change. Troubled, King recognized fierceness and restlessness in their faces—a bitter anger that, to his bafflement, seemed to be directed at him.

"Gonna walk on de water?" It was one of the young black men shouting derisively at King.

King's disciples inched in closer to him.

A second young black man cried out mockingly, "De Lawd!"

A third stepped off the sidewalk, advancing toward the marchers. "Uncle Chicken Wing!" he shouted.

From the opposite side of the street came another taunt. "Uncle Chicken Wing come all de way down here to save us!"

Bernard Lee, agitated, crowded in so close from behind that he stepped on one of King's heels, causing him to skip a step. Annoyed at himself, Lee dropped back a pace.

"Tell us about freedom now, Uncle Chicken Wing!"

For a second there was a look of hurt in King's eyes. Then he blinked it away.

Other young black men were leaving the sidewalks, stepping out into the street.

"You have a dream, King?" one of them called derisively.

"Tell us about your dream!" yelled another.

Suddenly, behind King, there was shoving. The hecklers from the sidewalks had moved in among the marchers, and one of them thrust himself between Bernard Lee and King. Lee grabbed at him and missed. The young man butted into King from the rear, knocking him forward. King stumbled, reaching out, then he was on the pavement on his hands and knees.

The sight of Martin Luther King on his knees in the street, struck down by a black man, brought cries of indignation from the crowd. The march halted, breaking up in confusion. As King's aides helped him to his feet, Bernard Lee gripped the attacker's arm with one hand; his other hand had hardened into a fist, cocked.

"Leave him alone," King admonished softly, as he got to his feet. "Leave him alone."

Lee had no chance to argue. There was a crash, the sound of a window breaking. Shouts and screams rose from the crowd; from somewhere ahead came another smash of shattering glass. The marchers broke away, some of them running. More windows broke. There was an edge of panic now to the voices of the shouters in the crowd.

Reverend James Williamson came hurrying up. A local black leader, gray-haired and in his early forties, Williamson was doing his best to stay calm. He reached out to stop a fleeing marcher, but the man tore free and ran on. Williamson gestured futilely.

"What's going on?" Andy Young demanded.

Williamson had been at the front line of the march. "It's going to be all right," he assured Young. "There's some trouble, but we'll get it under control."

Bernard Lee, who had released King's attacker and was watching him disappear into the confusion, turned at the sound of Williamson's voice. "It's going to be all right!" he repeated furiously. "It was going to be all right from the beginning!"

An explosion cut him short. Gunfire!

Bernard Lee and Andy Young pressed in close to King, becoming shields.

"We're getting him out of here!" Lee said sharply to the others, urging King forward.

King resisted.

"Let's go, Doc!" Lee snapped.

"Maybe it will be all right," King said, looking hopefully at Reverend Williamson.

But Lee had made up his mind; there would be no further delay. "It's *not* going to be all right!" he insisted. "I'm taking you out of here!"

Still acting as shields, Lee and Andy Young hustled King away, with Ralph Abernathy and Larry McKeecham clearing a path for them. The sweetly acrid odor of tear gas hung in the air now. The shouts and screams had become wails of anguish. The crowd shoved and cursed. Men fell and, as they scrambled to rise, were knocked flat again in the crush.

A car, nosing its way hesitantly through the throng that filled the street, nearly hit Bernard Lee, then stopped.

Lee shouted at the driver, a black man, through the closed window, "We have Dr. King here! Can we use your car?"

For an instant the man seemed undecided, then, nodding, he began unlocking the car doors.

As Lee opened a rear door, a black man of about thirty came hurrying toward the car, his eyes fixed on King. Andy Young quickly turned and faced him, blocking his advance, but in this case, the caution proved to be unnecessary.

"I'm Detective Redditt," the stranger said, flash-

11

ing his badge. "Follow me. I'll get you through."

Young and Abernathy got into the rear seat of the car with King positioned between them, and Lee and McKeecham squeezed into the front seat with the driver. With Detective Redditt leading the way on foot, the car began a slow crawl through the crowd. The tear gas, diffusing, was settling over the area like a mist. Through it, those in the car could see the police clearing a space in front of a section of stores.

"Is that where the trouble was?" the driver asked. "What happened?"

"We don't know," Lee answered, peering out the window. "We heard shots."

"There—on the sidewalk!" Young exclaimed.

They saw a black man stretched out on the cement. Around his limp, lifeless body the police were brandishing clubs, driving back those who had not fled, the curious and concerned who were trying to get close enough to see who the dead man might be.

King leaned across Ralph Abernathy, looking out the car window. He peered steadily at the figure lying dead on the sidewalk as the car continued its snail-like crawl through the crowd. In his expression was sorrow and self-recrimination, as if he were blaming himself for the death and rebuking himself for deserting his fallen compatriot.

The car broke free of the crowd; then, sent off with a slap on the rear by Detective Redditt, it sped up the street. Bernard Lee spoke once, to give directions to the driver; otherwise there was silence in the car. There were questions to be asked, but no one present could answer them. They could only ponder and grieve.

Shortly the car pulled up and parked at the entrance to the local Holiday Inn. While Andy Young lingered to thank the driver, Lee, McKeecham and Abernathy hustled King into the motel, across the lobby, and up the stairs. Not until they were in King's room did they dare relax their wariness. They shared the sense, sharpened by experience, that they were never more than a half-step ahead of peril.

"Martin, you better get some rest," Abernathy said gently. "God only knows what comes next."

Bernard Lee agreed. "You want to be sharp," he said.

"You'll find out what happened?"

"We'll get on it," Lee promised.

King's shoulders sagged as he entered the bedroom. Abernathy followed him to the door and closed it.

A few minutes later, Andy Young rejoined them, accompanied by Reverend Williamson.

"Well?" Bernard Lee demanded.

"The boy's dead," Young replied.

They were not surprised.

"How did it happen?" Abernathy asked.

Young shrugged his shoulders. "The usual thing. Some say he attacked the police. Others say he came out with his hands over his head." He made a face of disgust. "What happened? Who knows?"

Bernard Lee confronted Williamson. "You told us it was all in hand," he said bitterly. "We prepare for these things, you know."

"It *was* all in hand," Williamson protested. "I

don't know what happened. I've never seen most of those men who were pushing King."

Young eyed him narrowly. "What do you mean you've never seen them before?"

"I mean what I said. I recognized a couple of them. Most of them, though, I've never seen before. I don't know where they came from."

Young scowled, partly suspicious, partly skeptical. Then he addressed Abernathy. "Where's Martin?"

Abernathy nodded in the direction of the bedroom.

Young went to the door, opened it a crack, and looked in. King was asleep on the bed in his underwear. Young entered quietly and covered him with a blanket, then returned to the main room.

"I've never seen him so depressed," Abernathy said, as Young emerged from the bedroom.

Larry McKeecham looked up. "He's got plenty of reason to be depressed. Can you imagine what they'll make out of this?"

"It's more than that," Young returned wearily. "It's another death. Another black man dead. That's what weighs on him." He sighed. "It's a heavy load to carry."

The others nodded glumly.

The news was on television the next morning when King came out of the bedroom, dressed and ready to travel. Andy Young was stacking suitcases near the doorway. Bernard Lee was on the phone, talking to the desk clerk. King moved as if magnetized to the TV set and stood watching the screen, his expression flat, emotionless. The news clip, a

14

coverage of yesterday's march, showed him being hurriedly convoyed by his aides through the panicking crowd. Then the image on the screen changed. Adam Clayton Powell, the black Congressman from New York, was being interviewed by a newsman.

Smiling smugly, Powell was saying, "It never struck me as particularly moral to let people hit you without hitting back. The tenure of Martin Luther King's leadership of the black people is over. As a matter of fact, I have a nickname for him: Martin 'Loser' King."

The picture changed again. The scene was a Senate corridor. A Senator named Byrd was making a statement.

"Yesterday," Byrd was saying, "the nation was given a preview of what may be in store for this city caused by the outrageous and despicable riot that Martin Luther King helped to bring about in Memphis, Tennessee. If this self-seeking rabble-rouser is allowed to go through with his plans here, Washington may well be treated to the same kind of violence, destruction, looting, and bloodshed. When the predictable rioting erupted in Tennessee, Martin Luther King took off like a scared rabbit."

The tenseness in the room was almost tangible, but King registered nothing. Once more the scene changed. Stores were being looted. The sound track crashed with gunfire and shattering glass.

There was a knock at the door. Andy Young opened it to two porters, middle-aged black men.

"Martin—time to go," Young said.

King switched off the TV.

15

"Let's not miss that plane," Bernard Lee agreed briskly, hanging up the phone.

"You Martin Luther King?" one of the porters said, awed.

King smiled, nodding, looking embarrassed.

"You know what we call you at home?" the second porter said. "Little Lord Jesus."

Lee touched King's arm, urging him toward the exit. "Ralph and Larry are waiting downstairs," he said. "We better get going."

"Let me shake your hand," the second porter pleaded, as they approached the doorway.

King grasped the man's hand when he reached him. "I thank you," he said quietly. And he held the hand for a long moment, as if somehow he hoped to receive a recharge of strength and conviction from the man's touch. Then, preceded by Bernard Lee, the point man, and trailed by Andy Young, the rear guard, he moved on, unrejuvenated but returning to battle nevertheless.

2

The King house in Atlanta's black ghetto was modest and middle-class in size and design. Inside and out it was well-kept. Clearly, its occupants had a considerable respect for cleanliness and order. Indoor plants, carefully tended, suggested an appreciation of and a compatibility with nature. A sudden burst of musical laughter, a youngster's, indicated that the respect for order did not rule out moments of uncontrollable giddiness. The furnishings, still sturdy but well-worn, manifested unequivocally that comfort and familiarity took precedence over style and fad. All in all, it was a house of human warmth.

Coretta King, the wife of Martin Luther King, Jr., stood at a window in the living room, staring out, seeing nothing. She was an attractive woman, with a graceful bearing and compassionate eyes and a manner that bespoke a quick intelligence. She seemed to be listening for some sound that she expected to come from far off, and her stillness was intense, as though she were afraid that if she made any sound herself, if she even sighed, she might not hear it.

Across the room from her, seated on the sofa,

was Martin Luther King, Sr. He was in his seventies, but he looked younger by at least ten years—as if, for the past decade, he had managed to keep age at arm's length. He was not a large man, but the restless vigor he exuded and his commanding demeanor created the illusion that he was a giant in many ways.

He was not only father to the family, but father to his whole congregation. He was a moral force that even white men in the community feared when it was unfashionable to be at all concerned about the moral strictures of a black man.

Rising, King senior growled impatiently. He looked about the room as if he were looking for something to smash.

"Why don't you go up to him?" Coretta said calmly, still facing the window.

"They're destroying him, aren't they?" His tone was savage. "I knew they would—and they're doing it."

"Dad, you've got to control yourself," Coretta soothed. "You can't let him see that you feel this way."

"How can you use nonviolence with such brutes!" The words were clubs. "Such bastards! You've got to stand up to them!"

Coretta remained outwardly calm. "Why don't you go up and ask him to come down?"

"I can't. He doesn't listen to me any more." The old man gestured in frustration. "I can't. I can't go up to see him. I have a beautiful son and they're destroying him." He looked sadly at Coretta, who was still facing away from him, then sighed and

18

crossed toward the doorway. "Destroying him," he said, leaving the room. "I knew they would."

Coretta stayed at the window for a while, standing motionless, hearing her father-in-law's voice coming from the kitchen, angrily railing against his son's enemies one minute, against his son's faith in nonviolence the next. She felt sorry for her father-in-law; it was not easy for him, having a son who had chosen to turn the other cheek rather than to exact an eye for an eye. At last the house grew quiet again.

Slowly Coretta climbed the stairs. At the door to the bedroom that she shared with her husband, she paused and listened. No sound came from inside. Quietly, she opened the door and looked in. Her husband was seated in the easy chair by the window, preoccupied. He gave no sign that he was aware of her presence. On the floor at his feet was a newspaper, its headline shouting the news of the death of the young black man in Memphis.

"It isn't your fault," she said softly.

He looked up. "Yes, it is."

Coretta stepped in and closed the door. "How can you say that?"

"We shouldn't have allowed one person to march in that protest who didn't accept nonviolence. We should have understood the depth of those young people's bitterness toward me."

"Martin," Coretta said, sitting down on the edge of the bed, "you can't be responsible for every demonstration that goes wrong all over the country."

"Did you hear what Byrd said on the floor of the

Senate? That I was responsible for people being killed."

His pain was not audible in his tone, but she felt it, felt the familiar anger at injustice. She shrugged: "Since when have you cared about what he said about you?"

"It isn't only him. It's the others. It's our young people that hurt the most."

She looked at him closely. "Are you going to Louisville?"

"I've missed two flights." He paused, then continued wearily, "I know why I missed those flights. The ones who are waiting for me . . . I don't have anything to say to them. . . ."

"Martin, they're the people who have always attacked you. They're the ones who never fought until you spoke up. They all want to be Martin Luther Kings. They're not offering anything constructive. You know that. You know what they are."

He looked at her levelly, his eyes dark and unreadable. "Maybe we should let them have their way," he said. "Maybe we should let violence take its course. I know it's wrong. I know it isn't going to work. But maybe it has to be."

She was shaken. "Martin, you've never talked that way!"

"I've never been this tired," he said, looking away.

Coretta started to speak again—but she was distracted by conversation from downstairs. Listening, she recognized the voice of Andy Young.

"Is that them?" King asked.

"I think so . . . yes. . . ."

"Tell them," he said.

"All right, I will."

Coretta rose. She touched her husband's cheek affectionately, then left him, closing the door behind her, and descended the stairs.

In the living room she found the four men who had been in Memphis with him—Andy Young, Ralph Abernathy, Bernard Lee, and Larry McKeecham. With them were two others, Neal Price and Stanley Levison. Price, a black leader from the Midwest, in his middle twenties, was a restless, aggressively impatient man. Levison, white, considerably older than Price, was a New York lawyer, one of King's closest advisors. Levison had the look of a man who, even while at war with formidable foes, could remain at peace with himself.

"Is he coming down?" Andy Young asked Coretta.

She shook her head almost imperceptibly. "No."

There was a second of silence.

Then Neal Price said, "The way he's been acting the last few days, maybe it's just as well."

"What about the Poor People's March?" Andy Young wondered aloud. "It becomes all the more important now."

"All the more important to drop," Price said edgily.

Stanley Levison disagreed. "He's got to go back to Memphis," he said. "He's got to prove that nonviolence isn't dead."

"*Why* does he have to prove it?" Larry McKeecham asked sourly.

"We know you never believed in it," Abernathy responded.

"You're damn right I never believed in it. As a

tactic, I went along with it," McKeecham said. "But believe in it? What kind of idiot do you think I am?"

There was a pause, during which the silence grew uncomfortable. Then Levison addressed Andy Young. "The Poor People's March won't be anything without him," he said. "What do you think? Will he be able to make it? How is he?"

"How do you expect him to be?" countered Young. "Twelve years he's been at it. The man's exhausted."

Twelve years, Coretta thought. Could all of that activity, all the horror and pain and jubilation—be contracted into twelve years? It was beginning to seem like a lifetime. Yet Andy Young was right, it had been only a dozen years. A little more than a decade of trying to change what had existed for centuries.

As her husband's associates continued to discuss the problems that his exhaustion had raised, Coretta ceased to hear the specifics of their conversation. It became a background drone, an accompaniment to the recollections of the past twelve years that filled her mind. She looked across the room at the framed photographs on the wall. There was the picture of her husband with President John Kennedy and his brother Robert. Next to it was the photograph of Martin, his father, and herself with King Olaf of Norway, taken when her husband had been presented with the Nobel Peace Prize.

To the heights of adulation, she thought, and to the depths of abuse and humiliation. Her mind replayed a vivid memory: Martin being wrestled down a street in Montgomery, Alabama, by a pair of white policemen, his arms twisted cruelly behind his back. Again she saw the vicious faces of the policemen—and the face of her husband, serene, as, by force of will, he kept himself from showing the pain, denying the policemen the satisfaction of knowing how much they were hurting him.

She wondered if he would have set out on the journey of those dozen years if he had known at the outset what the cost would be. What kind of man was he? She was closer to him than any of the others, she knew, and she could have answered the question in a hundred ways. Yet she could not be completely sure what it was that drove him. Seeking the answer, she thought back to the beginning, to the year 1952, when she and Martin had first met.

3

Coretta, age twenty-four, a student at Boston University, sat at the piano in the tiny Boston apartment that she shared with another student. She was playing scales, practicing. Even at this age there was something noticeably out-of-the-ordinary about Coretta. Those who were slightly acquainted with her remarked on her ladylike grace. To know her better was to realize that her graceful demeanor emanated from a calm maturity, a confidence in herself, and an appreciation of the worth and sensibilities of others.

The phone rang.

"Gloria, can you get that?" Coretta called out to her apartment-mate, who was seated in the one easy chair in the room, a book on her lap, studying.

"It's for you," Gloria answered, as the phone rang again.

Coretta peered at her, puzzled. "How do you know that?"

"Just a guess," Gloria said innocently.

Still mildly perplexed, Coretta left the piano and picked up the phone.

"Hello?"

A male voice said, "This is M. L. King, Jr."

From the chair, Gloria whispered, "Be nice to him."

On the phone Mr. King continued, "A mutual friend of ours—Gloria, that is—said some very wonderful things about you."

Coretta glared at her friend, who giggled and hid behind the textbook.

Into the phone Coretta said, "Oh, yes. M. L. King . . . I've heard some nice things about you, too."

"I'm a little cynical about women," he returned. "But from what Gloria tells me, you're about to restore my faith."

Dryly, Coretta said, "Well, isn't that nice. And a little surprising, since you haven't even met me."

"Your reputation precedes you," he declared. "Every Napoleon has his Waterloo, and I have a feeling that I'm about to meet mine."

"Just a second, please . . ."

Covering the mouthpiece, she narrowed her eyes at Gloria, who was peeking out over the top of her book. "Is this a joke?"

"He's nice," Gloria insisted. "I just told him about you, that's all. Talk to him. What's the harm?"

Shaking her head in dismay, Coretta removed her hand from the mouthpiece.

"Yes . . ." she said. "I'm back."

"Now, when am I going to be able to see you?" King wanted to know.

She was hesitant. "I don't know. . . . My evenings are pretty full this week."

"How about lunch?"

"Well, I'm free from twelve to one—between classes."

"I'll meet you on the Huntington Avenue side tomorrow. I have a green Chevy. It usually takes ten minutes to make the trip to B.U., but tomorrow I'll do it in seven."

"Fine. Until tomorrow, then."

Coretta hung up. "It's nice of you to try to play Cupid for me," she remarked to Gloria, returning to the piano. "It would be even nicer, though, if you'd let me know about it in advance."

"I thought I was doing you a favor," Gloria sighed. "Haven't you ever heard of M. L. King, Jr., son of Martin Luther King, Sr.?"

"Who's he?"

"Which one?"

"Both," Coretta laughed.

"Martin Luther King, Sr., is the most well-known minister in Atlanta," Gloria told her. "He's on the board of the first black bank there. And his son is— Well, his son is his son."

"Oh? And what does his son do?"

"He's studying to be a minister, too," said Gloria, looking hopeful.

Coretta winced. "That's all I need—a Baptist preacher."

When she finished her last morning class the next day, Coretta strolled over to the Huntington Avenue side of the university. As she approached a corner, a green Chevy pulled up a short distance away. The young man who got out of the car and approached her was short and dressed in the traditional black silk suit of the Southern Baptist minister. Outwardly, her expression of polite, friendly greeting remained unchanged, but inwardly, she was registering her first impression of M. L. King,

Jr.—and deciding that she had made a date for lunch with a teen-aged dandy.

"Coretta?" he said warily.

She nodded, smiling, amused. "How old are you? Eighteen?"

"I'm twenty-three," King answered defensively.

"I'm twenty-five," Coretta informed him, emphasizing the "five"—apprising him, in as kindly a fashion as possible, that the difference in their ages was an insurmountable barrier to any relationship more intimate than sitting across from each other at a lunch table.

King was not in the least daunted. "I age fast," he told her. "Maybe I'll catch up."

In the green Chevy, they drove to the university cafeteria. When they reached the end of the line, Coretta's tray was crowded with small plates piled high with food.

"I'm glad you don't have a delicate appetite," King said as they set down their trays at the table he had chosen. "I like people who like food. But how do you keep your figure?"

"Well, to be truthful, what I usually have for lunch is peanut butter and graham cracker sandwiches," she confessed. "My expense money doesn't cover big lunches."

"Oh . . ." he said, understanding. "Have you tried the pecan pie?"

Coretta shook her head.

"They have *good* pecan pie," he asserted, rising.

"No, please . . . don't bother."

But he was already on his way back to the counter.

Looking after him, Coretta re-evaluated him. He

was rather nice, she decided. But peculiar. A theory occurred to her. Perhaps he wore the black silk suit as a label, a badge of identification; it was possible that without it he wouldn't know what or who he was. On the other hand, it was equally likely he knew who he was and didn't care much for the identity, and so wore the black silk suit like a masquerade costume. Whichever, she suspected, it was a disguise.

When King returned a few moments later, he was carrying a large slice of pecan pie.

"Thank you." She smiled as he placed it before her.

For a few minutes they ate in companionable silence. She *was* hungry, and she sampled her smorgasbord with relish.

"It's a pleasure just to watch you eat," he remarked.

"Now, you're making me self-conscious."

"I'm sorry." He changed the subject. "Where you from?"

"A small town outside Marion."

"Where?"

"Heilberger."

King suddenly grinned, then laughed.

"What's so funny about it?" she wondered, curious.

"My favorite story is about Heilberger," he said.

"Oh? What is it?"

"Well," the future minister began, already smiling in anticipation of the punch line, "there's these two guys from Heilberger, see, and they steal this pig. They're in this car, making their getaway, and a police car comes along and pulls them over. So the first guy says, 'What are we going to do about the pig?' And the other guy says, 'Put your hat on it.'

"So a cop comes over to the car and says, 'Let me see your license boy.' All this time, the guy in back is trying to keep the pig quiet, but the pig is making all kinds of noises. So the cop looks in back, and he says to the guy, 'What's your name, boy?' The guy tells him. Then the cop looks at the pig and says, 'And what's your name?' For once, the pig is quiet. So, the guy in back gives the pig a poke, and out comes a grunt. So the cop walks back to where the other cop is waiting, and he says, 'You know sumpin'? I know niggers are some ugly goddamn creatures, but you know what? There's one nigger sittin' in the back over there named Oink. That's the ugliest, blackest damn nigger I ever seen in my life.' "

"What are you majoring in?" he asked after a moment.

"Performing arts."

"Gloria says you're studying music. What do you want to be? Another Ella Fitzgerald?"

"No, I want to be a concert singer," she replied seriously, looking up.

"That's wonderful," he said enthusiastically. His smile returned. "I never met a concert singer."

"I'm not quite one yet."

"Where have you sung?"

"I gave a concert in Marion." She paused, then, shyly, "They . . . seemed to like me."

He was quiet for a second, studying her, she thought. Then he said, "It must take a lot of courage to say, 'I'm going to be a concert singer,' and then go at it and do it. What made you decide?"

"I went to see Paul Robeson," she replied. "He was wonderful. He came to Antioch." Her expression became thoughtful, then was creased by lines of fretfulness as the circumstances came back to her. "There were people in the town who were frightened to go see him. They were afraid they might be thought of as Communists. Can you imagine that," she asked, bewildered, "missing a chance to see and hear Paul Robeson because of his politics?"

She was aware that King was looking at her with a new interest. "So you have other things on your mind besides music?"

"Well, of course. Did you think I wouldn't?"

His only answer was a smile. Coretta realized what he had been thinking, though: that, being female, she would have a one-track mind, and, thus, if she were concentrating on music, she would be totally oblivious to everything else.

When they left the cafeteria, Coretta still had a few minutes to spare before she had to be at her next class, so she allowed herself to be driven idly around the campus in the green Chevy.

"You know," her date said, a second or so after the drive began, "I'm probably going to marry you."

She looked at him sideways. "What are you talking about?"

He shrugged, accepting the inevitable. "It's probably just the way it's going to happen."

"I'm glad you think so," she said tightly, "since you don't even know me."

She knew what he was going to say next, and he said it.

"You have everything a man could ask for. Beauty, courage—"

She interrupted. "Listen. Please don't think you have to heap all those ridiculous compliments on me. I'm not a silly little girl. I'm a grown woman."

"And you are beautiful. Don't you think you are?"

"No, I don't."

"I don't understand," he insisted. "You *are* beautiful. That's a fact. Why does it bother you so much to hear somebody say it? Don't you like being beautiful? Has it hurt you in some way or some thing?"

"Oh . . . I'm just tired of being on exhibit, an experiment," Coretta said. "That's what I am here at the university, an experiment. You know what it's like. Everybody tells you how nice you are, that you're an exception, and asks you why other colored people can't be like you."

"Aren't you making too much of it, though?"

She was silent for a moment. Then, "Things happen," she said. "There was a Jewish boy from Wheeling. He seemed to be different."

"Serious?"

"No. We were just good friends. Then one day a bunch of us got into a station wagon to go to a music festival near Wheeling. When we got to the city limits, he called his folks, and we were supposed to have dinner with them. I asked him if he had told them that I was a Negro. He said, 'What for?' "

"If you're not black, I guess you don't know 'What for,'" King said quietly.

"We went to a restaurant," Coretta continued. "We had to go upstairs to a special room because I was with them." She looked out the car window, off across the campus, seeing the scene in her mind again. "I saw his courage evaporate. He decided that they didn't have room enough at his family's house to put us up for the night. He didn't have the guts."

"Nothing new about that."

"I know I'm going to have to put up with this the rest of my life," she said bitterly, "but I'm never going to get used to it. And nobody is ever going to make me believe that it's right."

"No," he agreed. "Never feel it's right."

The words were quiet, but there was an undertone of strength in his voice. She faced him again. "Has anything like that ever happened to you?"

"Well, I was pretty secure in Atlanta. My dad is a hero there. But . . . yes, it happened to me. I went home with a white boy one day after school. His mother wouldn't let me in the house because I was black. It was a shock."

"Oh, well . . ." she said, dismissing it. "You'll get along all right. Ministers always do."

He glanced at her. "You don't like clergymen very much, do you?"

There was anger in her tone when she replied. "Maybe it's just the ones around my home that I resent. They're always more worried about their parishioners' souls than if they have enough to eat."

"Is *that* all you don't like about them?" King sounded surprised. "What about their cowardice?

33

What about the way they uphold the status quo? What about the way they turn religion around and make it just the opposite of what it's supposed to mean?"

Coretta looked at him, startled. She'd never heard a clergyman talk that way before.

Before she recovered, King said, "Arthur Rubinstein's giving a concert at Symphony Hall this Friday. Can I take you?"

"Well . . ."

"You may not like me—me being a minister's son"—he smiled—"but you're bound to like the music."

She smiled in return. "All right," she agreed.

"Friday, then?"

She nodded and set quickly off across the campus. She had a feeling that King was watching her, but she wasn't sure whether she was pleased or displeased about it. He confused her. He dressed like a dandy, and the joke he had told her was crude and insensitive—yet he had made some remarks that showed substance and compassion. Which one was the real M. L. King, Jr.? she wondered, taking her seat in the lecture hall.

Well . . . it didn't matter, she decided. The Rubinstein concert would probably be the last she would ever see of him.

4

It was a sedate and polite party, held in the home of one of the black students at the university. Most of the guests were students from either the university or the conservatory. They stood about in small groups and pairs, talking quietly, smiling plastically. The only disruptive noises came from the two young ladies who were engaged in conversation with M. L. King, Jr. Every once in a while the girls would break into giggles, which they would immediately stifle, embarrassed about drawing attention to themselves.

A few paces away, Coretta stood near the piano, half-listening to a young man tell her why she could never have a successful career as a concert singer (because concert music was "white"). Coretta made appropriate responses, but she'd heard the argument before; her attention was on King. She was remembering that several weeks earlier she had told herself confidently that her acquaintanceship with the minister's son would be short-lived. Since then, they had been together almost every evening. And Coretta was troubled. There were more and more signs that the relationship was becoming serious, but spending her life as a

Baptist minister's wife was not in her plan for herself.

When the young man who had been advising her to forget about a career in concert singing excused himself, she focused her full attention on the give-and-take between the two girls and King.

"My father heard your father preach a sermon at Ebenezer Baptist Church," the girl named Beatrice was saying to King, "and he said it practically changed his whole life."

King's eyebrows went up. "Drove him out of the church, did it?"

Dutifully, Beatrice giggled.

"M. L., where do you get your clothes?" the girl named Lara asked. She turned to Beatrice. "M. L. always looks like he stepped right out of a bandbox."

But King had caught Coretta's glance, and making his excuses to the girls, he moved to join her.

"You enjoy them clustering around you that way, don't you?" she said, amused.

"I enjoy it very much," he admitted.

Coretta looked past him toward where the two girls were still standing. "Beatrice is very beautiful," she remarked.

"Very beautiful," he agreed. "The most beautiful girl I ever saw."

She looked at him curiously. "Then why did you bring me here?"

"I wanted you to see that there are some girls who can't resist M. L. King, Jr.," he said. "With you, I was beginning to think I'd lost my touch."

She laughed. "Maybe these girls don't know that

there's a rumor around that you're engaged to a girl in Atlanta."

"I am."

"Then why did you say that you're probably going to marry me?"

His eyes met hers. He said levelly, "Well, I hadn't met you when I got engaged."

Coretta laughed incredulously. "Why do you want to be a preacher?"

King smiled. "I come from a whole line of preachers. My father's a Baptist preacher, my grandfather's a Baptist preacher, I have an uncle who's a Baptist preacher, and my brother is studying to be a Baptist preacher."

"That isn't a very good reason."

"Want some punch?" He went to the refreshment table, poured a glass of the pink fluid from the tureen and brought it back to her. "Just because religion isn't used the right way doesn't mean it can't be."

"How can it be used?" asked Coretta, surprised at the intensity in his voice.

"You talked about Paul Robeson," said King, "and you worked with the Progressive Party. But to really carry out the precepts of Jesus would be the most revolutionary and dangerous thing in the world."

Coretta laughed at the grandiose nature of the statement. "You going to try it?" she asked.

"I'm just a middle-class preacher's son," said King. "But if anything's going to start with our people, it's going to have to be through the church."

"What do you mean?"

"It's all our people have. It's all they can call their

37

own. It's the only place where somebody is going to be able to reach them."

"You've thought about it a great deal, haven't you?" said Coretta, looking at King with more and more surprise.

"Yes," he said quietly. "I know exactly the kind of congregation I want to have. It has to be a large one so that it has an impact on the community, and it has to be in the south."

"Why the south?" asked Coretta, astonished.

"Because that's where I'm from. Because it's where they need me most."

It was a moment before Coretta spoke. "It seems a pity. You're so bright. It seems you would be able to do almost anything you want to do. Down there you'll be just another black man."

"Look at these guys," said King, gesturing around the room, indicating the students. "They're the most improbable white men I've ever seen."

She laughed.

"They're running away—running away from everything they are." He faced her again. "I can't run away from the south and what I am, and the people I've known all my life. I want to be a good pastor. I have no other ambition. I like pastoring."

Coretta saw a great deal of King in the next few months. She found herself sharing and enjoying things with another person in a way that she had never thought possible before.

One night when he had come to her room, it came to a head. They were embracing, and he felt her hold back.

"What's the matter?" he asked, puzzled.

She said, "I could never be the kind of wife you want. I'll be your girl—while school lasts. Then . . . then we'll go our separate ways."

"I feel too strongly about you. Don't you feel that way about me?" He crossed the dark room slowly, moving toward the windows. "Could you take it if we separated?"

Tears filled her eyes. "Oh, Martin! You're asking me to give up my life," she said wretchedly. "Everything that's important to me."

"Sometimes things aren't easy," he agreed. "The last thing I need in the world is an emancipated woman who wants to sing with the Metropolitan Opera Company. But . . . sometimes life doesn't give you any choice."

"But you do have a choice," said Coretta. "You always have a choice." Her whole life had been based on that.

King looked out of the window into the night. He was silent for a few seconds. "Maybe you're right," he said finally. "Maybe we should stop seeing each other."

Coretta looked at him, startled.

"I'm going to Atlanta next week. Come with me to meet my folks or I'll never see you again."

Coretta realized that this was a challenge, a gauntlet that this gentle man, the most gentle man she had ever met in her life, had thrown down to her.

Seated in the front pew of the Ebenezer Baptist Church in Atlanta, Martin beside her, Coretta observed Martin Luther King, Sr., at work. In the pulpit he was an awesome presence, his voice, as he preached, conjuring up images of thunderbolts and lightning.

"The Bible," King told the congregation, his voice booming, "refers to prayer about five hundred times. It refers to faith *less* than five hundred times. But it speaks to us about material possessions more than *one thousand* times." He paused to let that point sink in. "We wonder"—he brought it home—"if anyone ever said to Jesus, 'Lord, you emphasize money to much!' "

From the congregation came contrite murmurings.

"Now, I asked you to sign your names on the envelopes you put your contributions into," he ent on. "And I've been checking up on you." He canned his audience. "Mr. Perkins—"

From the rear of the church came the sound of restless scuffling.

"Mr. Perkins, you think a man with the business you have can only afford to give fifteen dollars?"

The slightest murmur breathed through the congregation, and a male voice in the back responded with an apologetic mutter.

The Reverend stepped away from the pulpit, his eyes scanning the worried faces. Then he singled out another parishioner. "What about *you*, Mr. Washington?"

A tall, well-dressed man who was conspicuously seated in the front pew replied sheepishly that he would be more generous in the future.

Later, in the study at the rear of the church, King senior was introduced by Martin to Coretta. "I understand you're a singer," he said.

"That's right."

"You know 'There Is a Balm in Gilead?'" he asked, seating himself at his desk.

"I'm studying to be a concert singer," she returned, annoyed at the note of defensiveness in her voice.

"Concert singer." He made no effort to conceal his disapproval. "The only way you can help my son with singing is to sing in the choir."

"I don't intend to sing in the choir," she informed him flatly. "I'm going to have my own career."

King senior made a long face. He turned to his son. "Have you talked to her about that?"

"What about Adam Clayton Powell and Hazel Scott?" Martin reminded him. "They seem to get along all right."

"You ain't Adam Clayton Powell," King senior informed him. "And you," he told Coretta, "ain't no Hazel Scott that I can see—yet." He leaned back in his desk chair. "How well do you know this young man?"

"We've known each other a few months." Her voice sounded strange to her, strained.

King senior turned and looked at his son. "He'll give his last pennies in his pocket to a beggar coming along in the street if you don't watch him. Do you know *that* about him? He doesn't understand that money is freedom."

"It can be," she agreed. "It can also make you a slave."

Her answer surprised the Reverend, who looked at her as if he were actually seeing her for the first time. He came very close to smiling, and there was the merest hint of softness to his tone when he addressed her again.

41

"He's gone out with some of the finest girls, you know. Beautiful girls. Intelligent. Fine families."

"I'm sure he has," she replied politely.

"He gets serious every other week."

Coretta glanced quickly at Martin. He had a hand over his mouth, hiding a smile. He was obviously enjoying the grilling she was getting from his father.

"We love people," King senior continued, his tone softening a bit more, "and we want to be nice to everyone." He lowered his eyes. "But we don't know how to act."

"It must be difficult for you," Coretta allowed, wondering where this was leading.

He looked at her levelly. "There's one girl . . . a girl from one of the finest families in Atlanta. We've grown to love that girl. She has a lot to offer."

Coretta faced him squarely. "I have something to offer, too."

When they left the study, Coretta and Martin went for a long, idle walk, mostly for the purpose of giving Coretta a chance to work off her indignation.

"You didn't say a *word* during all that!" she complained bitterly when they were out of earshot.

"What good would it have done?"

None, she conceded. "I don't know if I'm going to be able to go along with this," she said heatedly. "He embodies in one person everything I'm trying to run away from. That sermon! And the way he talked to me!"

"He's a tyrant, all right," Martin agreed amiably. "But he's a lovable tyrant."

"I don't find him so lovable."

"His father was a sharecropper. One of my

42

father's duties when he was a boy was to curry the mule. Ever been around mules much?"

"Of course not."

"He used to go to school with the smell of the mule and the mule's hair still on him. The kids would make fun of him. He'd tell them, 'I may look like a mule. I may smell like a mule. But I don't think like a mule.' He came to Atlanta with fifteen cents in his pocket. He married the daughter of the most prominent minister in town." Martin laughed. "Not only that, he wound up taking over the congregation."

She was not amused. "I don't find that so admirable."

"Well . . . let me tell you something else about him," he said quietly. "He's also never ridden in the back of the bus or let anyone call him 'boy.' And he's done more to break down segregation than any other clergyman in town."

"Then why don't you marry *him!*" she retorted crossly.

Martin halted. "Coretta," he said, when she stopped, "I know his faults as well as anybody else—maybe better. I've seen him turn my brother into mush because he won't do what he says. I've watched him dominate my sister's life. But he's my father, isn't he? I can't change that, can I? And I love him. I love him very much."

"I understand that." But that, in a sense, was what worried her. "I just wonder. . . . Are you sure he won't dominate you?"

Martin shook his head. "*Nobody's* going to dominate me, Corrie. I'm not going to prove anything to him, though, by standing up to him and showing him how wrong he is. Time will prove him wrong. And when that time comes, he'll be big enough to admit that he's wrong.

Some months later Coretta found herself sitting in the living room with King's mother, Alberta—a wonderful, charming, kind woman—and his sister, Christine, younger than Martin but with a great maturity and a great feeling for people. They were listening to the sounds coming from the study, where the voice of Martin Luther King, Sr. was considerably louder than his son's.

Trying to make Coretta feel better, Alberta said, "It must be difficult for you to go to school and work at the same time."

"No, it's not so difficult," said Coretta, still trying to listen to the voices coming from the other room.

Alberta watched her for a moment, then said, "Have some more coffee."

The door opened. King senior appeared, followed by Martin. "Right," he said, addressing Coretta. "You're going to be in the family."

Astonished, Coretta looked up at Martin, who was smiling at her. She then turned to King senior, who sat without saying a word. Resenting him in spite of herself, she stared at him. At last, not looking at her, not looking at anyone, he said stiffly, "I accept you because you're his choice. I respect his opinion and his choice."

5

It seems incredible to believe now that there was a time, and not too long ago, when blacks, when boarding buses in Montgomery, Alabama, were requested to pay their fares, go to the back of the bus, sit in a special section, and then give up their seats to white people if the bus got crowded. But that's the way it was, and not too long ago.

People say that Rosa Parks did what she did because she was a member of the local NAACP. Others say that she did it because she was tired. There is a word called *zeitgeist*. It means destiny and time. Destiny had tracked down Rosa Parks in Montgomery, Alabama. The indignities of her life had tracked her down. She had simply had enough.

On that first day of December, 1955, Rosa Parks found herself last in line. Waiting, she watched the others board the bus, pay their fares, then get off and file back to the rear door where they climbed on again.

Rosa paid her fare, but refused to go to the back. Instead, she went directly to a row where two black women and a black man were seated. She sat behind them.

A white man came hurrying up. Reaching the row in which Rosa had settled, he stopped and stared; there were no seats available except farther back in the bus. The man waited, then looked toward the driver.

"You-all better make it light on yourselves," the bus driver called back. "Let me have your seats."

The three black people in the row with Rosa stood up and moved to the rear. Rosa did not budge.

"You gonna get up?" the driver said threateningly. He shook a warning finger at her. "I'm gonna call the police and have you arrested!"

"Go on and call them," she replied calmly.

Rosa looked at the black passengers seated around her. Some of them were in sympathy with what she was doing. Others simply looked away. Still others looked at her with hostility for causing trouble that might involve them, too. Rosa sighed tremulously and was ashamed of herself for doing so.

When the policeman came on the bus, he had two uniformed officers with him. Looking uncomfortable, the officers confronted Rosa Parks.

"Did the driver ask you to stand up?" the first one asked.

She nodded. "Yes."

"Why didn't you get up?"

She met their eyes steadily. "You think it's right that I should have to stand up after I got on the bus and took a seat?"

The two officers exchanged looks of embarrassment.

Then the first policeman addressed Rosa again. "I don't know about that. But the law is the law."

He looked down at the floor. "You're under arrest."

He took Rosa's handbag; the other policeman took her arm. They led her off the bus to a police car, and drove toward the city jail.

Jack Corbin, a traveling salesman who had long been active in the affairs of Montgomery's black community, stood before the clerk in the city jail to pay bail for Rosa Parks. Corbin was known as a fighter for civil rights, and an eccentric. The truth is that Corbin had little tolerance towards most of the black people in Montgomery. Maybe that was because his business of selling to black people all over the country had carried him outside Lownes County and taught him an emotional fact that people living within Lownes County didn't know. The fact was that no man is better than anybody else.

When Corbin walked out of the clerk's office, someone called to him from outside the jail. Looking out, he was startled by what he saw. There was a group of black people standing by the door.

"What happened?" a man asked him.

"They found her guilty," Corbin said. "I'm going to have to make bond for her. I'll bring her right on out."

"You don't bring her out, we'll come in and get her," said the man.

Corbin looked with wonder at the people standing in the street.

It wasn't the first time, or even the hundredth, that black people had been beaten, humiliated, and thrown off buses. Last year, they had beaten and put in jail a fifteen-year-old girl because she didn't want to give up her seat. These people had sat still for it all. Now they were telling him, Corbin thought with wonder, that if he didn't bring out Rosa Parks, *they* would come in and bring her out.

That evening, there was a meeting of the Montgomery Improvement Association at the Dexter Avenue Baptist Church.

A committee of blacks, mostly clergymen, had assembled. Ralph Abernathy was there. Also present was a relative newcomer to Montgomery, the Reverend Martin Luther King, Jr. Corbin, who had arranged the meeting, called it to order. After a cordial greeting to the assembly, he reported that he had arranged for bail for Rosa Parks; then he asked what progress had been made with the plan for the boycott.

Abernathy spoke up. "I've got the pamphlet here. It's all set."

"Let's hear it," Corbin said.

Abernathy read aloud, "Another Negro woman has been arrested and put in jail because she refused to give up her bus seat. Don't ride the bus to work, to town, to school, or anywhere else on Monday. If you work, take a cab or share a ride or walk. Come to a mass meeting Monday at seven p.m. at the Holt Street Baptist Church for further instructions."

There were comments of approval.

"Whose names go on it?" one of the clergymen asked.

"No names have to go on it," another responded.

"Don't they?" Corbin said icily.

48

The Reverend Cox stood up. "This is a secret committee," he said. "Nobody knows we're here except us. White people don't have to know who the members of the committee are. That way no one gets hurt."

"That way nobody gets hurt, huh?" Corbin paced a few steps, then turned abruptly to face them. "Who's gonna pay any attention to a pamphlet with nobody's name on it? Where are they gonna think it came from—out of the sky?"

"You advertise a secret committee," Cox pointed out, "and it's not a secret anymore."

"For years," Corbin said with emotion, "washwomen have been putting their money in the church, and you people have never done a damn thing for them."

The men muttered resentfully.

A gesture cut them short. "*Now* is your chance," said Corbin. "This committee has got to come out of hiding. You got to stand up and make yourself known. You got to have a leader—a president for this committee." He pointed. "My choice is right there—Reverend King."

King, surprised, laughed nervously. "Why me?"

Corbin's tone was matter-of-fact. "I've thought about it a long time. And you're the one to do it, you're gonna be the president."

"Mr. Corbin, I just came here to a meeting, not to be picked for anything," King protested. "I don't think I'm the one you want. Remember, now, I've been in this community for less than a year."

Corbin allowed him a half-smile. "That's why.

The establishment hasn't had a chance to get to you—yet."

King laughed again. "Is that the best reason you can think of?" He shook his head. "That's not enough."

"You're also one devil of a speaker," Corbin said.

"Mr. Corbin," King said, "things are pretty hectic at my house right now. My wife just had a baby. Besides, I'm starting some new programs in my church. That takes time . . . and—"

Corbin interrupted. "You turned down the chance to be president of the NAACP here, too," he said, looking at King speculatively. "What's the matter with you?"

"Nothing's the matter with me," King replied edgily. "I just feel that other people are more qualified."

Corbin turned to face the entire committee again. "What do we have here, anyway, a bunch of scared boys or grown-up men? You know what they say about you preachers? They say all you're interested in is what's in the collection plate. Are they right?"

There was silence for a second.

"I'm not a scared boy. I nominate Reverend King as president," one of the clergymen announced.

The vote was unanimous.

6

Quietly opening the door to her husband's study, Coretta peeked in. King was at his desk, writing.

"How are you doing?" she asked.

"I'm paralyzed," he said, looking up. He motioned to her. "It's all right . . . come on in . . ."

She closed the door and crossed to him. "Worried?" she asked. "I don't know why. You're a good speaker. You're the best speaker I know."

"I've got to be careful," he said, as she sat down in the straightbacked chair beside the desk. "It'd be easy to let my Baptist fervor run amok . . . tell them 'Go out and fight!' And then what? The same kind of violence will break out here that's broken out everywhere else, and things will return to what they were before—and *worse* than before. It's easy to give that kind of speech."

"What would you like to say to them?"

He pondered for a moment. "I'd like to talk to them about all the things that you and I have talked about a thousand times. I'd like to tell them about Thoreau's essay on civil disobedience . . . and about Gandhi and the power of unearned suffering and the use of nonviolence." He smiled ruefully. "But this isn't a seminar. It's people who haven't had a chance to have any education. I have to talk to them in their terms, not mine." He looked at her levelly. "I'm inadequate to do it," he said.

"Then—" She stopped, at a loss. She knew he was wrong, of course, knew that the committee could not have chosen better, but understood as well the tremendous pressure this placed on him.

As she hesitated, there was a knock at the door.

"Yes?" he called out.

The door opened and Jack Corbin entered, excited. "It's time to go, Martin," he said. "There's a crowd around that church two blocks long."

"I haven't finished my speech yet," King objected.

Corbin shrugged. "You'll have to finish it on the platform. This won't wait. This thing is big. Reporters are there—some of them from up North. Television! Martin, they've got television cameras in the church. You don't need a speech. Just open your mouth and let God speak for you."

King followed Corbin out the door.

When they reached the church, the crowd in front was so large that they had to enter through the rear. There they were met by the members of the committee, who crowded around them, barraging King with last-minute advice. He seemed not to be listening. His mind was on the sounds of restlessness coming from the people who were gathered in the church.

When he entered the pulpit there was an immediate hush. King squinted, reacting to the glare of the television lights. Then, as his eyes adjusted to the brightness, he scanned the auditorium. Every seat was occupied. The aisles were jammed. People were packed into the doorways. He began to recognize faces ... Ralph Abernathy ... Rosa Parks. ...

"We are here," he said quietly, beginning tentatively, "because of the bus situation in Montgomery. We are here also ... because of our love for democracy ... because of our deep-seated belief that democracy, transformed from thin paper to thick action ... is the greatest form of government. ..."

"Yes, sir! That's right!"

"And we are determined—"

"Determined!" a woman shouted.

"—to apply our citizenship to the fullest extent of its meaning."

"Yes, sir! That's right, brother!"

"On so many occasions," he went on when the noise subsided, "Negroes have been intimidated and humiliated and oppressed ... because of the sheer fact that they are Negroes."

"That's right!" a man agreed.

"Just the other day, one of the finest citizens in Montgomery"—he paused—"not one of the finest Negro citizens—"

"Oh, no!" a woman affirmed.

"—but one of the finest *citizens* in Montgomery ... was taken from a bus and carried to jail ... and *arrested*—"

"Arrested!" the crowd cried out.

"—because she refused to get up to give her seat to a white person!"

From all sides came the shouts:

"Yes!

"Yeah!"

"That's right!"

"Yes, sir, brother!"

King emphasized the point. "Just because she refused to get up, she was arrested!"

"Arrested! Yes!"

"You know, my friends," King said, speaking softly, "there comes a time . . . when people get tired of being trampled over by the iron feet of oppression."

The crowd erupted in a wild cheer, an explosion of suppressed rage. The walls of the church seemed to tremble. King, startled by the reaction, appeared frightened for a second, as if he doubted his ability to channel the powerful force that his words had released. He raised his hands to quiet the cheering. But it continued, its volume swelling. And, responding to the roar, King seemed to grow, in stature and in strength.

Gradually the cheering abated.

"There comes a time," he told the crowd, his voice strong, "when people get tired of being pushed out of the glittering sunlight of life's July . . . and left standing amidst the piercing chill of an alpine November."

Again the crowd cheered.

"We are here this evening," King said, "because we are tired *now!*"

"Tired!" came the litany. "Yes, sir!"

"My friends . . . don't let anybody make us feel that we are to be compared in our actions with the Ku Klux Klan . . . or with the White Citizens Council . . ."

"No!" a woman shouted.

"We are not advocating violence!" His tone made it a command.

"No, sir, no!"

"There will be no crosses burned at any bus stops in Montgomery! There will be no white people taken out of their homes . . . and taken out on some distant road . . . and murdered."

"No! No!" they agreed.

"My friends . . . I want it to be known . . . that we are going to work with grim determination . . . to gain justice on the buses in this city."

"Oh, yes, brother!"

King leaned forward in the pulpit. When he spoke again, his voice was a trumpet. "And we are not wrong, we are not alone in what we are doing! If we are wrong, the Supreme Court of this nation is wrong!"

"Yes! Yes! Yes!" the crowd roared.

"If we are wrong . . . the Constitution of the United States is wrong! If we are wrong . . . God Almighty is wrong! If we are wrong, Jesus of Nazareth was merely a utopian dreamer and never came down to earth! If we are wrong, justice is a lie! And we are determined here in Montgomery to work and fight until justice reigns!"

The crowd cheered hysterically, shouting, stomping. Tears of joy and pride filled the eyes of the young girls, the mothers with children, even the men. King, his arms upraised, had to gesture again and again and again to quiet them.

When he was able to speak once more, his manner and voice were subdued. "When the history books are written in the future—"

"Yes, sir, in the future."

"—somebody will have to say there lived a race of people—"

"Yes, sir!"

"—of black people—"

"Yes, sir! Yes, sir! Black people!"

"—who had the moral courage to stand up for their rights . . . and who injected a new meaning into the veins of history and civilization . . . and we are gonna do that! God grant that we will do it before it's too late!"

Once again, the assembly erupted in a cheer of such force that the building seemed to shake. The people came surging forward, swarming around the pulpit. King found himself being pummeled with backslaps and deafened with cries of praise and congratulations. Stunned and immobilized by the response, he had to be rescued by members of the committee.

The next morning King and Coretta stood in the street, watching one bus after another roll by with only white people inside.

"They're empty!" Coretta said to King. "They're empty!"

Three weeks later, another man noted that the buses were still empty. He was Damon Lockwood, an elegantly dressed black man in his 30s from New York. Observing beside him was Stanley Levison, a white man also in his 30s, casually dressed, as though he did not care about how he looked, but with a gentle, inquisitive manner.

Looking at the empty buses, Damon thought it should have been obvious to anyone from the beginning that if black people could be united anywhere, it would set off an explosion. The fear of losing their jobs, the fear of ostracism from even their black neighbors, had divided them. Now black people were walking to work, and the boycott had lasted for three weeks. Martin Luther King, whoever he was, had worked a miracle.

7

It was a fairly typical moment in an ordinary weekday afternoon at the King house in Montgomery. King was in the kitchen, talking with members of his congregation. People felt free to wander in any time, to have dinner, to contribute breakfast, just to sit and talk with King. Coretta, who had just finished bathing the baby, Yolanda, was patting her dry with a thick towel. Mr. Giddings, a parishioner, a man near sixty, was exploring in the refrigerator, looking for leftovers that might strike his fancy. Another parishioner, Mrs. Boson, who had brought chitlins for King, was now advising Coretta on the care and feeding and proper bringing-up of babies.

Carrying Yolanda, who was now wrapped in the towel, Coretta went to answer a knock at the door. She found two men there, one black, one white. The black man, rather elegantly dressed, had sharp features and a questioning expression. The white man was more casually outfitted. He had a set, stubborn look about him.

"Mr. Lockwood!" Coretta said to the black man, recognizing Damon Lockwood, a well-known writer and lecturer.

He was surprised. "Do we know each other?"

"I met you at Antioch," she told him. "You came to speak. I sang for you later. You were very encouraging."

"Yes . . . of course . . ." he responded vaguely, obviously not recalling.

"Pardon me for the way I look," she apologized. "I was giving the baby a bath."

"Yes, I see." He indicated the white man. "This is Mr. Levison . . . Stanley Levison."

"How do you do," Coretta said, smiling cordially.

"Is Dr. King here?" Lockwood wanted to know.

"Yes," she said, and invited them in.

The two men entered, then stood looking about the kitchen. At the table, Martin was reviewing a speech while he ate, and he had not heard Coretta admit the newcomers. At last Lockwood addressed him. "Where is Dr. King?" he asked.

Martin looked up from his notes, smiling. "I'm Dr. King."

Lockwood seemed doubtful for a second. "You photograph older than you look in person," he said, but extended a hand and again introduced himself and Levison.

King offered a hand to Levison. "How do you do."

"Mr. Levison is a veteran of the labor movement," Lockwood explained. "He wants to help us. We're both down here to see what we can do to help. This movement has accomplished something that no movement in the South ever has."

Mr. Giddings, turning away from the refrigerator for a moment, raised his eyebrows in interest. "What's that?" he asked Lockwood.

Lockwood glanced at him, frowned irritably,

then directed his answer to King. "It's been obvious to everyone right from the beginning."

"The President coming down here?" asked Mrs. Boson, accepting it matter-of-factly. She had seen enough bizarre happenings since the beginning of the bus boycott to believe anything was credible.

"No, of course not," replied Lockwood. "But the mere fact that you're asking him will be news."

"What are your plans?" Levison asked King, taking a chair across from him at the table.

"The mayor and the council have asked for a meeting," King replied. "I think we'll find some kind of accommodation."

"Don't be surprised if it doesn't work out that way," Levison said sympathetically. "People don't give up their privileges unless you force them to."

"Well, we'll try it." King pushed back his chair and got up. "Pardon me. I have to get ready for the meeting."

Mrs. Boson called after him as he was leaving the kitchen. "Glad you enjoyed the chitlins, Dr. King."

He halted in the doorway to give her a smile. "Mrs. Boson, I think you make the best chitlins in the whole wide world."

She beamed ecstatically.

"Ironic, isn't it?" Lockwood said later to Levison, when they were alone together.

"What?"

"That this hayseed should have the power to move these people this way."

Levison smiled wryly. "Are you sure that's all he is?"

"Aren't you?"

61

"I don't know." Levison shrugged. "People have a disquieting habit of surprising my assessment of them all the time."

"Did you see the way he was attacking those chitlins?"

Levison narrowed his eyes in reproof. "That sounds a little racist, Damon."

"Does it?" Lockwood made a face of mild dismay. "Maybe I am. I'm black, but I've never understood my own people. What other people would have stood for this and not fought back? They're almost saintly. And to be saintly is stupid."

"There couldn't be a little jealousy in your assessment of Reverend King, could there?" Levison suggested.

"Of course there is," admitted Lockwood. "I've spoken in half the universities of the world. I know every phase of black history and exactly what should be done. And I can't reach them and move them the way he can."

Entering the chambers of the city commissioners, where the meeting was to take place, King and his associates were surprised to discover that the session was being covered by the local television station. The lights and the unblinking eyes of the cameras added to their discomfort as they took their places at the conference table. They were tyros at the game of negotiation. Never before had the heads of the white establishment consented to a meeting with a delegation of blacks. Now it appeared that they must not only engage in a difficult confrontation, but they must do so while exposed to the glare of the critical public eye.

Mayor Burchett, the other representatives of the city, and the spokesmen for the bus company were already seated at the table. One of the whites was Mrs. Lucille Jackson, a member of one of Montgomery's most aristocratic families. Another was Louis Herbers, a self-proclaimed racist, representing the White Citizens Council. For the clergy, there was Dr. Wendell Ballard, handsome and white-haired. The others were Mr. Wicker, attorney for the bus company, a Mr. McComb and a Mr. Prial, both of whom, so far, had taken a moderate stand in the conflict.

"Who is the spokesman?" Mayor Burchett asked when the committee members had seated themselves.

There was a second of indecision. Then the other members of the boycott committee turned their eyes to King.

"All right," Mayor Burchett said. "Come forward and make your statement."

King glanced at the television cameras, uneasy. Then hesitantly he rose. He was bothered by the brightness of the lights and intimidated by the generally grim expressions of resistance on the faces of the whites at the other side of the table. He was suddenly aware of how young he was and how inexperienced at this kind of confrontation.

"We have three requests," King said, his voice somewhat shaky. "One. First-come, first-served seating arrangement, with Negroes loading from the back and whites from the front." He cleared his throat. "Two. A guarantee of courtesy from the bus drivers. Three. Negroes to have jobs as drivers on predominantly Negro routes."

Silence.

King sat down.

McComb, one of the moderates, spoke. "That seems reasonable enough," he said.

"I don't see how it can be done within the law," Wicker, the bus company lawyer, objected. "I would be the first to go along with it, but—but it just isn't legal."

"If we granted the Negroes these demands," Louis Herbers put in, "they would go about boasting of a victory they had won over white people."

King drew in his breath. In the uncomfortable pause that followed he turned to the mayor. "I object to the presence of Mr. Herbers, a member of the White Citizens Council," he said. "How are we going to make progress with a man who admits he's a racist?"

The mayor shrugged. "He has as much right to his point of view as you have."

"I object to the implication of Dr. King's remarks," Mrs. Jackson said, bristling. "He's saying that this council is meeting with a closed mind."

"As a matter of fact," the mayor said smoothly to King, "there are people in Montgomery—black people—who think that your role as spokesman is the main reason for this boycott not being settled."

Once more there was silence.

King looked to the left, then to the right, expecting support from his fellow committee members.

The silence lingered.

A look of hurt flickered in King's eyes.

At last, leaning forward at the table, Ralph Abernathy addressed the whites. "Dr. King represents the Negro community of Montgomery," he stated clearly, leaning hard on every word. "We have belief in him. He has our entire confidence. He speaks for us."

Relaxing a little, King smiled gratefully in Abernathy's direction.

"Well . . . we've heard your requests. . . ." the mayor said. "We'll certainly be willing to guarantee courtesy." He glanced at the whites around the table. There were slight nods of assent. "But we can't change the seating arrangement. Because such a change would violate the law. And, as far as bus drivers are concerned . . . we have no intention, now or in the foreseeable future, of hiring nigras."

Again, the silence. This time it indicated a stalemate.

"Dr. King . . ." It was the minister, Dr. Ballard, speaking. "I always thought the job of the pastor was to lead the souls of men to God. Not to get tangled up in petty social problems."

King stared at him in disbelief, astounded that a member of the clergy could refer to the conditions of oppression under which the blacks lived as petty social problems.

Half-turned toward a TV camera, Dr. Ballard continued. "I would like to remind Dr. King of his calling. I urge him and the Negro ministers to leave this meeting determined to bring the boycott to a close . . . and to lead their people instead to a glorious experience of the Christian faith."

King came home with the Reverend Ballard's words about Christian faith ringing in his ears. But there was something else ringing in his ears. His own failure.

Nobody was home except Stanley Levison, who was helping himself to some ice water from the refrigerator.

"Hello," said Stanley expectantly.

"Hello," said King. He went out into the backyard, and Stanley followed him. "How did it go?"

"Not so well," King replied.

Levison nodded. "I told you it wasn't going to be easy. But a Southern city council met with a black protest group for the first time. That's some kind of progress."

"The demands we asked for were so modest," King marveled. He sank down on a bench, searching, probing within himself. "The worst thing about it was that I felt like a fraud up there. I felt I wasn't equipped to speak. I felt I had no right to speak.'"

Stanley looked at him terribly moved.

After a moment, King said, "The first thing we're going to have to do to get anywhere, is to squeeze the slave out of ourselves. I know I haven't squeezed it out of myself yet."

Later, while King was at the church preparing for further meetings for the boycott, Coretta sat with Carol Lucy, a parishioner who often served as a baby-sitter for Yolanda. They were folding the baby's clothes when there was a thump on the front porch.

"Did you hear something?" Coretta asked.

Carol moved toward the front door. "Somebody's out there," she said. She called out, "Who's that?"

They heard a scraping sound.

Carol's eyes widened in fear.

"We better move to the back," Coretta gasped, retreating quickly. "Carol—come on!"

The two women hurried toward the kitchen, Coretta holding the baby tightly against her, shielding her with her arms.

As they left the living room, there was a tremendous blast. The force of the explosion hit them like a physical blow, knocking them forward.

At the Dexter Avenue Baptist Church, the meeting of the boycott committee was about to begin. King was standing near the speaker's platform, in conversation with Damon Lockwood and Stanley Levison.

Ralph Abernathy entered and hurried to the platform.

"Martin. They bombed your house!"

King, Abernathy, Lockwood, and Levison dashed from the church and drove to the King house. The street in front of the house was jammed with angry black citizens of Montgomery. When King got out of the car and was recognized, there were cries for vengeance.

The porch was a jumble of jagged-ended boards. King made his way through the debris and entered the house. He took Coretta and the baby into his arms, holding them tightly.

"The baby?" he said.

"She's all right," Coretta told him, struggling to control her weeping.

From the distance came the sound of a siren.

At the same time, the phone rang.

Still holding Coretta, King reached down and picked up the receiver.

A female voice said, "I did it! And I'm just sorry I didn't kill all you bastards!"

The line went dead.

King dropped the receiver back onto the cradle.

Outside, the mayor and the chief of police, having arrived in a squad car, were making their way through the crowd toward the house. Enraged blacks were shaking their fists at them, shouting threats. The mayor looked contrite. The police chief looked worried.

"Dr. King . . . we're sorry. . . ." the mayor said as he entered the house.

"It's a little late to be sorry," Lockwood told him through set teeth. He gestured at the damage done by the explosion. "This is the result of your 'get tough' policy."

Motioning in the direction of the crowd in front of the house, the chief of police addressed King. "Can you help us?" he pleaded. "If you can't, we're going to have to put in a request for the militia."

"*Now*," Levison said bitterly, "you're coming to Dr. King for help."

The crowd outside seemed to be growing.

"Will you come with me?" asked the mayor.

King looked at the mayor without speaking, then followed him to the door.

At the sight of him, the crowd cheered. He stepped out into the midst of the debris and raised his arms for quiet.

"How are your wife and child, Dr. King?" a man called out.

68

"We're with you, Dr. King!" another voice shouted, and several others seconded the support.

King spoke calmly. "My wife and baby are all right," he told them.

"We're with you, Dr. King! You're not alone!"

"If you're with me . . . then you'll listen to me. . ." King said. "If you have weapons . . . please take them home. If you don't have weapons, please . . please don't get any."

There was a murmuring of protest.

"I'm all right," King called over the noise. "My wife and baby are all right."

The murmuring continued, but was more subdued.

"Jesus still speaks to us across the centuries," King said. " 'Love your enemies. Bless them that curse you. Pray for them that despitefully use you.' Now . . . please . . . please go home. . . . We're all right." But King's voice rang hollowly, if only to himself.

"God bless Dr. King!" a deep voice cried out.

The crowd cheered again.

King lifted a hand, then turned and stepped back into the house.

A wiry young stranger followed him inside. "Dr. King, I'm Bernard Lee."

King looked at him absently.

Lee smiled warmly. "You don't remember me," he said. "I was in an Air Force uniform the last time you saw me. I came in late for the sermon; then, afterwards, we talked for a while." He nodded toward the bombed porch. "I'll stay here in case anything happens."

King winced. "I don't need a bodyguard."

69

"Yes, you do," Damon Lockwood said firmly.

"You need something else," said Jack Corbin, who had just arrived. "I sit in a rocker on the porch with a rifle in my hands. If anybody comes near the house, they know what to expect."

That night, in bed, King looked at Coretta and Yolanda, lying beside him. He put his arms around them, and the movement woke Coretta.

"Martin, what is it?"

"Nothing . . ."

"Tell me. What is it?" Coretta asked.

"They could have killed you and Yolanda," he said. "I'm trying not to hate. I'm trying to remember that it isn't all of them."

"I know," she said softly.

The next morning King did something he had never thought he would do. He went to city hall and applied for a license for a gun.

8

The impact of the boycott swept through the
south. In other towns, black people asked themselves: why had they lived this way? Why was it
necessary to live this way? One of them was Henry
Burroughs.

Burroughs had been waiting for a bus for a long
while. Alone on the dark street corner, he paced
back and forth impatiently. When at last he saw
the lights of the bus approaching, he grumbled
crossly to himself one final time, then shrugged
off the annoyance that had been building for the
last twenty minutes. With the bus in sight his anger
began to subside.

The bus reached the corner and stopped some
distance from the curb. The door puffed open.
Running into the street and stepping aboard, Henry
Burroughs became immediately aware of the in-
solence on the driver's face. To keep his irritation
under control, he kept his eyes lowered as he
paid his fare. He started toward the seats.

The bus did not move. The driver watched until
Burroughs was halfway back, then snarled, "Get
off the bus, boy, and come through the back door."

Burroughs stopped and turned, looked at him

squarely. "I will not go through the back door," he declared, returning to the front of the bus. The anger was fierce in him now. "I will get off the bus." He held out a hand. "Give me back my dime."

At that moment a uniformed policeman appeared at the bus door, which was still open. "What's the trouble here?" he asked.

"He won't get off the bus," the driver told the officer.

"Give me back my dime!" Burroughs raged.

The driver began getting up from behind the wheel. "You better get off this bus," he said brutally. His stance was threatening.

"Keep your hands off me!" Burroughs warned him, defiant.

"I'm telling you to get off this bus," the driver said viciously, grabbing for Burroughs.

The black man, quicker, gave him a shove, sending him stumbling backwards.

"I want my money!" Burroughs shouted. "Give me my money! You took my money!"

From behind, the police officer got hold of Burroughs and started to pull him down the steps. All of the suppressed rage that had built up in the black man over the years now exploded. Yanking free of the officer's hold, he gave him a push, then faced the bus driver again, his eyes flashing.

From the open doorway came the sound of a shot. Burroughs's body jerked convulsively and spun around as the bullet hit him. For a second he stared incredulously at the police officer and the gun in his hand. Then he dropped to the floor of the bus, dead.

A group of enraged blacks had gathered in King's living room. Some of them carried guns. "They have theirs guns," a spokesman, Parsons, declared. "We have ours."

King went to a drawer where he had locked up his revolver so that no one else could get at it. He took it out of the drawer. "You want a gun?" he said, thrusting it toward the others.

They looked at him, startled. "It's my gun!" King explained. "Take it! I don't want it! Take it! Take it!"

They were all stunned by the ferocity on the gentle man's face, and by his willingness to remain completely vulnerable though his house had been bombed and his wife and children nearly killed.

Later that day, King, Damon, Stanley, and Coretta were in the backyard drinking lemonade and playing with the baby when Bernard Lee ran up to them. "They've arrested Ralph!" Bernard said.

Lockwood looked at him incredulously. "Even segregationists couldn't be that stupid."

"What do you mean?" asked Coretta.

"If it's true," Lockwood explained, "it will make every front page in the country."

Lee turned to King. "They say they're going to have warrants out for all the leaders."

"Maybe we ought to go down there and help them get those warrants out more quickly," Stanley said dryly. "We can use all the publicity we can get."

"I'm afraid you don't know much about southern jails," Coretta interrupted, concerned. "Too often, when blacks go to jail down here, they just disappear. It may be good publicity, but don't think it isn't dangerous."

King went to one of the backyard benches and got his coat.

Coretta looked at him, alarmed. "Martin," she called. But King did not stop and she ran after him. The two of them walked together down the street.

At the courthouse, King tried to enter. There were two guards outside. "Where are you going?" one of them demanded.

"Inside," King informed him, replying amiably.

But the man had his orders. "We're not allowing no one in."

King's expression hardened. "I'm going in."

The defiance was unexpected. The guard looked at him curiously for a second, then shook his head. "You *can't* go in," he repeated.

"That's that King fellow," said the other guard.

"Get out!" the first guard now ordered.

King did not budge. His voice was even, but firm. "I am going in," he said, starting forward.

The guard put a hand on his chest, stopping him. "Boy," he threatened, "if you don't get the hell out of here, you'll need a lawyer."

King stepped sideways, then started forward once more.

"Boy, you done it now!" the guard exploded.

The two guards grabbed King. One of them twisted his arm behind his back while the other forced his head down, subduing him. They began hustling him from the courthouse.

"Let him alone!" Coretta cried out, following. "Let him alone!"

The guards stopped at the sound of her voice.

"You want to go, too, gal?" one of them taunted. "Just nod your head—that's all it takes."

"Darling, don't say anything," King begged her. "Go away."

"Martin!" she wept, struggling to follow.

At the jail, King was booked, then taken by two guards to an empty cell.

One guard kicked King in the leg, then tried to knee him in the groin. When, startled, he tried to protect himself, the other guard hit him in the stomach. Then the guards left quickly.

King kneeled on the floor in pain, trying to catch his breath.

In the city, the news of the imprisonment of King seemed to double the efforts of the boycotters. The buses remained empty. Car pools came into existence; cars passed with as many as twelve black people in them, sitting on each other's laps. Independent taxi companies were formed.

In one middle-class white household, a white employer asked her black employee, Mrs. Parker, if she wasn't tired of walking to work eight miles every day.

"My feets is tired, but my soul is rested," replied Mrs. Parker.

The day after his arrest, King found himself unexpectedly released. Stanley Levison was waiting for him outside the jail.

"I told you not to pay the bail," said King.

"I didn't pay it," replied Stanley, amused.

"Who did then?" asked King.

Stanley smiled. "No one would tell me, but I have a feeling that it was the police commissioner.

He must have felt that you were more dangerous in jail than out of it."

After a moment, King smiled too. He was thinking of something that Thoreau had once said: If one man in the state ceased to hold slaves and allowed himself to be locked in the county jail, it would have meant the abolition of slavery in America.

9

King and Levison sat together at the defense table in the courtroom. The court was not yet in session. As Levison hunched over the table, making notes on the case, King leaned back in his chair, staring into space, his expression sorrowful.

Behind them, in the public section, the seats were filling up, being taken mostly by blacks. Coretta was one of the earliest to arrive. Sitting down in the public section, in the seat directly behind her husband, she bent to speak to him, but seeing his look of weariness and despair, she sat back and composed herself. She would not trouble him now.

She watched as Fred Gray, a local black attorney who was working with Levison on the case, came forward. He and Levison consulted for a few moments, then Gray, too, began making notes. Now King leaned forward at the table. He looked steadily at the two lawyers for a minute or so, then spoke, addressing Levison.

"Stanley, where are we going?" he asked drearily. "Are we getting anywhere?"

Levison met his eyes. "Honestly, I'm not sure. But it's been almost a year, Martin, and the boycott is still on. That's *something*."

King nodded.

"Who thought it would last?" said Levison.

"But is it really doing any good?" King looked off into space again. "One of my parishioners told me something a couple days ago. She was walking to work, and a white woman stopped her. The white woman said, 'I see you doing this every day. I can't watch you any more. Aren't you tired?' My parishioner answered, she said, 'My feets is tired, but my soul is rested.'"

"Good," Levison said.

"I don't know—is it?" King sighed. "That was what I thought at first—it was a good answer. But now I'm starting to wonder. It's been a year, yes. The boycott is still on. But who's hurting? Not them. Us. We're the ones who're hurting." He gestured, taking in the courtroom. "Here, in the court, this is where they're hurting us. They've declared our car pools illegal. Here, in the house of justice, they tell us we can't bunch up in cars if we want to."

"We're appealing that, Martin."

"And how long will that go on?"

"I can't say."

"Now this case," King persisted. "They want us to pay fifteen thousand dollars for damage to the bus company. Damage. The damage is going to be to us."

"It takes time, Martin. The law works—"

The judge was entering the courtroom.

"All rise."

There was the sound of movement and shuffling as the lawyers, litigants, and observers got to their feet. Judge Carter, seating himself, declared the court in session. As the others sat down again,

78

Levison went to the bench to address the judge.

King felt a tap on his shoulder. Turning his head, he realized that a man, vaguely familiar to him, was handing him a sheet of yellow paper.

"I'm Conners, Associated Press," the man said. "Read that. It's what you've been waiting for."

King read. He grinned widely.

"What is it?" asked Fred Gray.

King handed the sheet of paper to him.

Gray's reaction was the same as King's, a face-splitting grin. Rising, he addressed the bench. "Your Honor, I have something here that the gentleman from the Associated Press has just handed us that I think has a bearing on this case."

Judge Carter nodded. "All right—what is it?"

Fred Gray read aloud, " 'The United States Supreme Court today affirmed a decision of a special three-judge United States District Court—in declaring Alabama's state and local laws requiring segregation on buses unconstitutional.' "

For a second the courtroom was silent.

Then a roar of jubilation rose up from the blacks in the public section. The judge brought down his gavel, demanding order. But the blacks, standing now, would not be restrained. The judge, realizing the futility of continuing to pound the bench with the gavel, tossed it aside.

The news had spread by the time King, accompanied by Coretta and his attorneys, emerged from the courthouse. A huge crowd of blacks was waiting. They shouted his name, cheering wildly. Standing on the courthouse steps, King responded with upraised arms. When they cried out to him to speak to them, he gestured for quiet.

"This morning," he announced when the cheering abated, "the long-awaited mandate from the United States Supreme Court concerning bus segregation came to Montgomery!"

The roar of exultation rose again.

"Listen to me! Listen to me!" King pleaded.

The crowd became quiet once more.

"In light of this mandate," he went on, "and the unanimous vote rendered by the Montgomery Improvement Association about a month ago, the year-old protest against city buses is officially called off."

"Praise the Lord!" a man shouted.

"And the Negro citizens of Montgomery are urged to return to the buses tomorrow morning," King told them, *on a nonsegregated basis!*"

His words were answered with a roar of triumphant joy that was like thunder. In the white sections of the city it shook foundations.

When Damon Lockwood and Stanley Levison called on King at his home a few days later, they brought along evidence of his growing influence beyond the borders of Montgomery. The first item was an advance copy of *Time* magazine, with King's likeness on the cover.

King stared at the picture of himself in wide-eyed surprise.

"Of course," Levison said, smiling, "there are drawbacks to that. I understand that J. Edgar Hoover has ordered a security check on you."

"Why?" King wanted to know.

Levison grinned. "You're a troublemaker," he explained.

Damon Lockwood held out another magazine.

This one was a comic book, with an idealized cartoon figure of King as a super-hero on the cover. At the sight of it, King winced.

"Martin, you're the first national black hero in this country since Frederick Douglass," Damon told him.

King tossed the magazines aside. "Heroes come and go," he said. "I'm twenty-six years old. By the time I'm twenty-seven, nobody will remember who I am."

"That doesn't have to be," Damon said. "We've been working out plans to gather all the Negro movements in this country outside the NAACP under your leadership."

King shook his head. "I'm not equipped to lead a movement like that," he said.

"What are you afraid of?"

King considered for a second. "I'm afraid of my own shortcomings," he said. He glanced at his likeness on the cover of the comic book. "I'm afraid that people will expect me to pull rabbits out of the hat."

"You don't have to worry about that," Damon reassured him. He looked at King narrowly, meaningfully. "We'll tell you what to do."

"No . . . if I'm going to be a leader it would be because I *am* the leader, no one else."

"Martin," Levison said gently, "no one person chooses a leader. People do. You might have wanted something else. We might have wanted to choose someone else. But it's what happened."

King looked away, unconvinced. "I'm a pastor first—and a leader second, if at all," he said. "I'll

81

go and speak anywhere you want me to. I'll write about my experiences. But, as for leading . . ."

"People think revolutions start with injustice," Levison said. "They don't. They begin with hope. Here you gave the people hope—and look what's happening. There are bus boycotts in Jacksonville, Nashville, Greensboro. There's even a boycott in Johannesburg, South Africa. Something has started. You may be the only one that can make it happen."

10

The cab was proceeding slowly but steadily through the heavy New York City traffic, heading for Harlem. In the rear seat were King and Stanley Levison. It was September, 1958, four years after King had been called to his first pastorate in Montgomery, Alabama. Now old friends, King and Levison were chatting casually about the days of the bus boycott. Suddenly King's manner changed. He sighed deeply, looking troubled.

"Four years . . . what's been accomplished? Not much, Stanley."

"You've traveled all over the South, you've spoken to thousands and thousands of people, you've written a book. That isn't exactly sitting back and resting on your laurels, Martin."

"I expected that Supreme Court decision to make a difference. But things are just about the same."

It was true, of course. Levison had no answer. "Well, you're doing what you can," he said.

"Black people disappear, murdered, and the police don't even ask questions," King said dismally.

"You couldn't expect that to stop just because we desegregated the buses in Montgomery."

"I was in Selma, Alabama, on voting day," King went on. "A black minister went to the courthouse to vote. The sheriff stood in the doorway. When the minister tried to go in to vote, the sheriff knocked him down. He got up and tried to go in again, and the sheriff knocked him all the way down the steps."

"Things like that have been going on a long time. You can't blame yourself."

King looked at him levelly. "What I blame me for is being a fraud," he said. "I go to these towns and I talk, and the black people gather 'round me . . . and I see hope in their faces. They think I can do something for them. I hear them talking. The women say, 'He looks just like Jesus . . . just like a little Jesus . . .' I give my talk, then I go away. I move on to the next town." He turned away, looking out the cab window. "I raise their expectations, then I leave them, and things are as bad as before."

"You can't do it for them, Martin. They've got to do it for themselves."

"But maybe if I stayed in some of these places long enough to get them started, maybe then they'd carry on and *do* something. But I'm in and out, in and out. I'm not giving myself, Stanley. I'm giving little glimpses. It's not enough."

The cab stopped, having reached its destination, a small department store in Harlem. Levison paid the fare and followed King into the store, where they were met by the manager, a middle-aged black man.

"I got you all set up in the shoe department," the manager told King, leading them through the aisles. "I got a big stack of your books, and we already got a crowd."

"Good," King replied vaguely, his mind obviously elsewhere.

The shoe department was astir with anticipation. A crowd of black people was gathered around a table that held tall stacks of King's book, *Stride Toward Freedom*. Catching sight of King, the people began calling out excitedly.

"Give him time!" the manager begged. "He'll sign every book. Give him room!"

A middle-aged black woman pushed forward. "Dr. King!"

"Yes," he answered distractedly.

"I've been waiting for you," she said, opening her purse.

There was a sudden reflection of light on metal. The woman raised her arm. In her hand was a steel letter opener. As another woman in the crowd screamed, she plunged the knife-like letter opener into King's chest.

More screams.

King stared blankly at the woman who had stabbed him.

Levison, who had become separated in the crowd, pushed forward and got hold of King.

Others grabbed the attacker and pulled her away.

"Get a doctor!" a man shouted.

"Get an ambulance!"

Stanley Levison eased King into a chair.

The well-wishers thronged around. At King's side woman reached for the letter opener, intending to remove it from his chest.

"No!" Levison said sharply, restraining her. "Let the doctor do it."

"Oh, Lord, oh, Lord!" an old woman wept. "Don't take him away! We need him!"

King's eyes were closed. He had lost consciousness.

Standing at a window at the end of a corridor in Harlem Hospital, Coretta looked down on the street, staring vacantly at the stop-and-go movement of traffic. Nearby, Stanley Levison sat slumped in an uncomfortable tubular steel chair. Occasionally he glanced up the corridor in the direction of the room into which King had been taken after surgery; then, seeing that the door was still closed, he sighed sorrowfully and faced forward again.

"Stupid . . ." Coretta murmured. "All he's done for black people . . . all he's *still* doing . . . and a black woman tries to kill him. . . . Stupid . . ."

"Not all black people see him the way we do," Stanley said. "Some, the only thing they see is that he 'stirs up trouble.' "

"Don't they understand—"

"No," he said sourly.

The door up the corridor opened, and the doctor who had operated on King came toward Coretta and Levison.

Stanley rose. "Here comes the doctor," he said to Coretta.

She turned from the window.

"So far, so good," the doctor said, reaching them. "The knife was touching the aorta. It's a good thing nobody tried to pull it out. We had to remove two ribs to get it free."

Coretta's voice trembled. "Will he be all right?"

"Yes—unless complications set in. It's so delicate. he'd sneezed, he would have died."

"Can I go in and see him?" she asked.

The doctor nodded. "But don't let him talk too much."

She hurried up the corridor and entered the room. Her husband was alone. His eyes were closed. He was breathing noisily because of the drainage tubes in his nose and throat. For a second she stood at the door and looked away, forcing back the tears that had suddenly filled her eyes. Then, in control of herself again, she approached the bed.

"Darling . . ." she said softly.

King's eyes opened. "Where have you been?" he asked weakly. "What took you so long?"

"I got the first plane out of Atlanta," she told him. "Don't talk."

"Why did she do it?" He seemed baffled.

"She said you were the Devil. She said she'd been told by God to get rid of you."

He closed his eyes again. "There are so many lies being told," he murmured. "There's so much hysteria. There's so much violence in this country. . . ."

"Please, darling, not now—don't think about it, don't talk."

"Stay . . ."

"Yes, I will," she whispered. "I'll be right here." His breathing became less labored. He was asleep.

The doctor came into the room, accompanied by nurse. "He'll be asleep for quite a while," he told Loretta. "There's no point in your staying."

"I promised him," she said.

87

The doctor shrugged. "You'll have to wait i
Reception."

"All right. But when he wakes up—"

"Yes, we'll let you know."

Levison was waiting just outside the door whe
she stepped into the corridor.

"How is he? What did he say?"

"He's asleep. He didn't say much . . . somethin
about the hysteria . . . the violence."

They walked toward the elevators.

"Hysteria breeds assassins," Levison said. "Some
where there may be another one waiting for him.
think he ought to go away."

"Run?" She looked at him. "He wouldn't do that

"I'm not talking about running," said Levisor
"He'll be a long while recuperating from this. Wh
not do it somewhere else, some other country?"

She shrugged. "I'm in favor of it. But I don
think you'll ever convince him."

He thought a moment. "There's one place h
might go. He's always wanted to go there. Th
would be the perfect time."

"Where?"

"India."

She brightened. "Yes—you're right. He admir
Gandhi so much."

"And Nehru invited him to India, didn't he

"Yes . . ."

"Well, then?"

"I'll suggest it," she agreed. She smiled, relieve
"I think he might do it. Even though Gandhi
dead, he might be able to do one more good wor
The memory of him may be strong enough to lu

Martin away from all this violence for a while. I hope so." When she raised her eyes again, Levison saw that they were full of tears. "I'm afraid for him, Stanley. I have the feeling that the next assassin won't miss."

11

When, after the attempt on his life, King was able to leave the hospital, Coretta suggested that while he was recovering, they accept the invitation of the Prime Minister of India, Jawaharlal Nehru, to visit his country. To her delight, he responded enthusiastically to the idea. Through the years, King's admiration for India's late spiritual leader, Mohandas Gandhi, had grown, and as Coretta and Levison pointed out, there could not be a better time to follow up his long-standing intention to make a pilgrimage to Gandhi's land. And so the trip was arranged.

In India, King and Coretta dined with Nehru. The two men talked at length about Gandhi and how greatly his philosophy of nonviolent resistance had influenced their lives. It was during that period of rest and recovery in India that King reached a decision about his own future. The conversation with Nehru, the sense of Gandhi's continuing influence, India itself helped to bring into focus his realization that he had a moral duty to accept the role of leadership that others in the black civil rights movement were urging on him.

Upon his return to Montgomery in late November of 1959, he was thus faced with the sad task of telling the members of his congregation at the Dexter Avenue Baptist Church that he was leaving them. Occupying the pulpit for the first time since his return from India, he scanned the familiar faces of the parishioners, feeling a surge of gratitude and love.

"I want to thank you for the letters and flowers that you sent me while I was ill."

There was a pleased, murmured response.

"As you know," he said, "Mrs. King and I went to India. We go to other places as tourists. We go to India, because of Mohandas Gandhi, as pilgrims. Gandhi teaches us that violence does not overcome evil; it suppresses it for the time being to rise later with redoubled vigor."

The parishioners nodded in agreement.

"Nonviolence, on the other hand, seeks to put an end to evil by converting the evildoer. In India we met Nehru, and Nehru said that Gandhi made one of his last public statements to a group of visiting American blacks. He said there was no dishonor in being a slave. There was dishonor in being a slave-holder."

The nods this time were more vigorous.

"But Nehru said that Gandhi said something else. Something most curious—that it may be through the American Negro that the unadulterated message of nonviolence is delivered to the world." King lowered his eyes. "A leader is demanded," he said softly. "I doubt whether I am that person. I have the gravest doubts."

The parishioners were beginning to realize that their pastor was not so much preaching a sermon as making an announcement. Some shifted in their seats to get a better view of his face.

"I must reorganize my personality and reorient my life," he said, raising his eyes. "I have been unfair to you. You need a full-time pastor."

There were whisperings now.

He smiled fondly at one of his parishioners, the elderly woman who had helped Coretta after Yolanda's birth. "Mrs. Boson," he said, "you need somebody to come from the church and see you when you don't feel well." He turned his eyes to a good-looking young man. "Jerry, you need somebody who is going to give you time in your meetings on civic issues." Then he faced the entire congregation once more. "I would like to submit my resignation as pastor of the Dexter Avenue Baptist Church, to become effective on the fourth Sunday of January."

There were cries of "No! No!"

"I must." He could say no more.

Mrs. Boson rose. Timidly she began to sing:

> "Blest be the tie that binds
> Our hearts in Christian love,
> The fellowship of kindred minds
> Is like to that above. . . ."

The choir joined in.

> "We share our mutual woes
> Our mutual burdens bear,
> And often for each other flows
> The sympathizing tear. . . ."

King bowed his head, his eyes wet with tears.

About to enter the bathroom of his home in Atlanta, Martin Luther King, Sr., found his son Martin standing at the sink, shaving. Martin was bare from the waist up, the ugly red scar along his rib cage showing.

"What did they do to you?" King senior exclaimed.

Martin glanced at him. "You know they had to take out a couple ribs, Dad." He resumed shaving. "I'm fine."

His father remained standing in the doorway. "Where did you get this nonviolence?" he asked gruffly. "You didn't get it from me. You must have got it from your mother. It's all right to turn the other cheek, but what do you do when you don't have any more cheeks left?"

Martin smiled, amused by his father's evaluation of the situation.

"You don't get things done the way you're going," the older man continued, working himself up into anger. "I've fought everything in this town, and I know what to do. You don't work from weakness. You work from strength." He indicated the scar. "And you protect yourself. You don't make yourself a target. It's better to be a live dog than a dead lion."

Rinsing shaving soap from the razor, Martin did not reply.

"Are you listening to me?" his father demanded.

"Sure, Dad, I'm listening."

"You're hearing, but you're not listening."

Martin changed the subject. "Dad . . . about working with you here at your church . . . Do you think your parishioners are going to understand that I won't be able to spend all my time on church business? We're getting the national movement going, and that will take most of my time." He began drying his face. "That's why I left Montgomery. I couldn't give the church my full time."

"Don't worry about my parishioners," his father replied. "They'll be glad to have you on any basis you want. You know that."

Martin put on his robe. "Your turn," he smiled, edging past his father, leaving the bathroom.

But King senior, annoyed that his son was not taking his advice seriously, trailed after him down the hall. "I didn't live to be my age by making myself a target for every redneck in Georgia," he growled.

"What are we having to eat, do you know?" Martin asked lightly.

"Eat!" his father erupted. "I'm talking to you—"

He was interrupted by the sound of the front door closing noisily.

"That sounds like that big noise, A. D.," Martin said affectionately.

A second later his brother appeared at the end of the hall. There was a general resemblance between A. D. King and M. L. King, Jr. The differences were that A. D. was a bit taller, a bit fleshier, and a great deal less confident in manner. At the sight of his father and brother, A. D. smiled sheepishly.

"It's a wonder you showed up," King senior greeted him gruffly.

"What's going on?" Martin wanted to know.

His father took a newspaper clipping from the pocket of his robe and handed it over. "He got in another fight." Turning to A. D., he snapped, "I told you—if you can't help us, don't hurt us."

Martin read the headline, which confirmed what his father had said, and returned the clipping. "One of those things," he said, dismissing the matter.

But King senior would not let the subject drop. "Look at you!" he said belittlingly to A. D. "I'm ashamed of you. I'm ashamed that you're a son of mine. I thought you were going on a diet."

A. D. shifted uneasily, his eyes lowered.

Martin laughed, trying to lighten the effect of his father's words on his brother. "You see, A. D.?" he jested, "if we're going to succeed in this world, we're going to have to have the brain of Einstein, the language of Ralph Bunche, and the looks of Marilyn Monroe."

A. D. grinned.

At that moment, fortunately, Coretta appeared in the doorway. "You're not dressed," she said to her husband, annoyed. "Come on, Martin. Mrs. Mazer just drove up."

He looked blank. "Who?" Then he remembered. "Oh . . . that real estate agent. Why now?" he protested. "We're going to eat."

"We have plenty of time," Coretta said. "The food won't be ready for another hour. Come on."

King shrugged resignedly. "All right. Just give me a minute."

A short while later, in the company of the real estate agent, King and Coretta arrived at a vacant house in Collier Heights, a middle-class section of the city. The house, a split-level, had the look of comfortable complacency. Coretta beamed at the sight of it. King grimaced.

"You're right, Mrs. Mazer, it's exactly what I had in mind," Coretta said to the real estate agent as they approached the house. "I always wanted to fix up a place like this for Martin—to make up for what he found on the road. It wasn't easy."

"Just wait till you see the garden," Mrs. Mazer gushed, opening the door. "It's out back. Right this way." She went in and stood aside to allow them to enter.

King got hold of Coretta by the arm, stopping her. "What are we doing here?" he said.

Coretta called out to Mrs. Mazer, "We'll be right along." The agent went toward the kitchen. Coretta faced her husband. "We have to have *some* place to live," she said.

At the door King gestured widely, taking in the large expanse of vacant living room. "We couldn't even pay for the drapes," he said.

"Your father says he'll make the down payment."

The real estate agent reappeared. "You said Dr. King likes barbecues," she said. "We have a built-in barbecue back here. Come and look. There's no harm in just looking."

They followed her through the house, then out the back door and into the garden. There, King held back again, while Coretta went with Mrs. Mazer to inspect the built-in barbecue. A few moments later, Coretta returned to where he was standing.

"What's the matter?" she asked, struck by the look on his face.

What she had never fully understood, up to this moment, was the depth of his hatred for that portion of the black middle class which had never helped the tremendous majority of dispossessed black people.

King looked out on the row of neatly manicured lawns of the Collier Heights people who took their vacations in Europe each year, who had swimming pools like those of the most affluent white neighborhoods.

"The black bourgeoisie, ripping off black people," he said. "Charging them all those fat fees for food. For doctor bills. For mortgages."

"Of course, that's the way they are," replied Coretta.

"Not in Collier Heights," King said. "I don't want it."

He strolled down the long lawn, so quickly that Coretta could not have kept up with him even if she had tried.

The next week, Coretta got a call from King telling her to meet him right away. He gave her the address of a house on Sunset Avenue, one of the poorest sections in Atlanta.

She arrived to find King standing with Bernard Lee before the house. "How do you like it, Bernard?" he asked. "Think we can find some way to improve it?"

"Doc, the only way to improve this thing is to dynamite it," said Bernard.

King looked at Coretta. "What do you think?" he asked cheerfully.

"Martin, it will take as much to improve this place as it would to live someplace decent," Coretta replied.

"I like it!" said King appreciatively.

Bernard and Coretta exchanged helpless looks.

12

Coretta was unpacking the cases, wondering how she was going to make the Sunset Avenue house look respectable.

In the other room were Julian Bond, looking younger than his 22 years, and other members of SNCC—Laura Jenkins, Jim Best and Jack Lake. Julian was talking to King and Stanley Levison.

Coretta had resented the attitude of the SNCC members when they first came in. They treated King as though he were an "Uncle Tom," this in spite of all he had done and tried to accomplish. King had warned her not to be intolerant of them.

Coretta tried to ignore them, but it was difficult, especially when they were trying to trap Martin into another one of their adventures.

"You know what Karr's Department Store is like," Julian Bond said.

"We don't think Dr. King should become involved in local fights," said Levison after a moment. He was acutely aware that he was the only white man in the room and that it might seem insolent of him to give advice on what to do.

"No?" said Laura Jenkins. She addressed King directly. "Does your father have too many friends here?"

Coretta paused in her unpacking with a sharp intake of breath.

"You speak about Gandhi," said Jack Lake.

That did it. Coretta charged into the room and addressed them all. "Don't you think my husband has exposed himself to enough danger? He's gone all over the country for SNCC, and you know it! When you get in trouble you call on him, and then when he comes you criticize him for taking all the publicity!"

"You know what happens in Karr's," Julian said quietly to King. His manner was not like that of the others. He did not share the contempt or the arrogance with which they addressed King, and he did not minimize King's achievements. "It's probably the best department store in town, and it degrades every black person that comes into it. Five restaurants, and we can only eat in the cafeteria. I took my nephew there to buy a suit. They don't let black people try on clothes for fear it might touch a white boy's body. They measured him with a ruler. Then a white boy came in with his mother. My nephew watched the white boy try on clothes and shoes. Watching my little nephew's face, I know it scarred him for life."

King didn't speak; he knew Julian's words were true. He looked at Julian.

Coretta looked away from King, knowing he would go.

Karr's is indeed a beautiful department store, as fine as any in the country. Entering the store with Bernard Lee, King walked quietly, aware of the pacifying Musak that filtered through the aisles.

King slowed his pace as he saw the line of student demonstrators outside the doors of the store's fancy restaurant. One of the students cried out, "It's King!" A cheer went up from the others.

King approached the hostess who stood at the restaurant's cashier's desk. As he did, he could not help looking at the diners. They seemed such respectable people, enjoying their lunches. There were women and their children, families who went to Karr's Department Store as an event, worth giving the kids a day off from school. There were women alone; they came to Karr's simply because it served one of the best lunches in town.

King stood before the pretty hostess. "I would like to be served," he said.

"We don't serve nigras here," said the hostess.

"I want to eat in this restaurant," King said.

"Here they come," Bernard Lee whispered at King's shoulder.

Police officers had arrived.

"You're trespassing on private property," a sergeant told King and the students. "I'm going to give you ten seconds to leave. One . . . two . . . three . . ."

"You know who this is?" one of the students asked the sergeant incredulously. "This is Martin Luther King."

The sergeant continued to count, unmoved. ". . . six . . . seven . . . eight . . . nine . . . ten . . . arrest the niggers!" He turned to the other officers. "Get the wagon!"

Inside the Atlanta City Jail, it was like a jamboree. Some of the demonstrators were singing

New Orleans jazz songs, others were arguing heatedly about the best direction for the Civil Rights movement to take.

King and Bernard Lee played Chinese checkers. "Wanna get beat again, Doc?" asked Bernard, as he won another game.

Suddenly a guard's voice rang out above all the others. "All right, everybody out except Dr. King."

The students looked anxiously at King.

"I'll be all right," said King, but he was not quite able to keep the wariness out of his voice.

"I don't leave without Dr. King," Bernard told the guard.

"I'm all right, Bernard." King put his hand on Bernard's shoulder. "Go on."

Back at the King house, the family was eating, taking it as a matter of fact that King would be coming home soon. Bernard entered and looked uneasily at the others as they ate. He seemed afraid to speak, as though he had done something wrong.

"Where's Martin?" asked Coretta matter-of-factly.

"He ain't out yet," said Bernard.

"Why not?" Tension rose in Coretta's voice.

King senior spoke impatiently, as though Bernard was at fault. "What's going on? Where's Martin?"

Bernard replied wearily, "I don't know. There's some kind of hearing going on."

At the hearing, Judge Mitchell sentenced Martin Luther King to six months imprisonment.

"The defendant is to be held without bail."

King's attorney rose to his feet. "Your honor," he

said, "you can't be serious about this. Six months for a *traffic violation?*"

The judge glared at him. "You seem to forget— Dr. King is on probation."

"Six months? For driving in Alabama with Georgia license plates?" the lawyer said caustically.

"He was warned after the incidents in Montgomery not to break that probation."

"Is either incident so serious, Your Honor?" the lawyer objected.

"I have a crowded ledger here," Judge Mitchell replied crossly. "I see no reason for giving your client special privileges."

The lawyer's hands, resting on the table, clenched into fists. "You're not giving him special privileges," he said tightly. "Quite the reverse. You're holding him without bail. Even a common criminal is allowed bail. Under certain circumstances, even a murderer is allowed bail."

"I have pronounced sentence."

King looked at the judge, trying to understand him.

"You'll allow us to draw up a habeas corpus?" the lawyer asked.

The judge nodded. "Yes—if you'll present it to the court in the morning."

In his cell later that night, King heard heavy footfalls approaching along the corridor. He peered through the dimness toward the cell door. The footfalls ceased; two dark shapes appeared outside his cell. The door was being opened. King steeled himself against another beating.

A light flashed in his eyes. A harsh voice ordered, "King! You're going to Riedsville!"

Held by the guards, King was hustled along the corridor. They entered a small, dimly lighted room. King could see the guards' faces now. They were young men. In other circumstances, both might have been considered pleasant-looking, but now their expressions were businesslike, compassionless. King heard a rattling of chains and realized that steel cuffs were being fitted to his wrists and ankles.

A guard shoved him, and he stumbled forward, the chains clanking. Then they had hold of him again and were pulling him and dragging him along another corridor.

He was shoved through another doorway and found himself out on the street. At the curb a van waited, its engine running. Suddenly he saw friendly faces. Several of the students who had sat in at the department store restaurant were standing nearby, watching. King understood all at once what was happening. To circumvent the possibility of having to release him on a habeas corpus the next day, the police were moving him tonight to another jail, perhaps delivering him to the chain gang. And his friends, suspecting that something like this might happen, were standing vigil.

One of the guards opened the rear doors of the van. King heard a low growl. Peering into the back of the van, he saw a wire mesh screen, behind which was an enormous German shepherd, snarling. Instinctively, King drew back. But the guards, lifting him, shoved him forward, rattling his heavy chains. One of the guards boarded the van behind him and pushed him into a seat. The doors slammed closed.

King heard the students shouting in protest.

Then the van was moving.

The cries of the students grew faint, then could no longer be heard.

In days to come, King would often talk to people about that ride in the prison van with the German shepherd. Only a black man who lived in the South in the 50's could truly understand what that ride had been like. Because in 1959 you knew they could take you out into the countryside and stand you by the side of the road and make you jump from a bridge, the way they had done it to Emmett Till.

In the van that night, King cried out that his cuffs were tight and were hurting him.

The guards were silent.

They were now riding along a narrow dirt road in almost total darkness. King looked out of the back window, the dog snarling at him. He could see nothing. "This isn't the way to Riedsville," he said. "Where are you taking me?"

The guards were silent.

But they did take him to Riedsville, and by the time they got there King was crying with relief that he was actually going to jail.

At the Riedsville jail, he was led down a corridor and pushed into a solitary cell. He sank back against the wall and slid down to the floor, tears still in his eyes. But now he was not crying with relief, but from the fear they had made him feel and the humiliation of that fear.

Coretta was trying to hold herself together by continuing to unpack the boxes for the house. Still, she was beside herself with fear. "I'm frightened," she said. "I'm frightened they'll find him somewhere on the side of the road."

King Senior watched her quietly. Nothing in the world mattered more to him than the welfare of his son. Yet he was able to help her at this moment. He spoke quietly and firmly. "Coretta, there are many things my son and I disagree about. But I admire his courage a great deal. All we can do now is the best we can for him—and try to live up to his courage."

Coretta was stunned by his dignity and courage. She began to understand fully why Martin loved him and where Martin had received some of his reservoirs of courage.

The phone rang. As usual, Yolanda was the first to answer it. "Hello."

"Yoki, get away from that phone," said Coretta.

Yolanda looked up at her. "It's someone that wants to speak to you."

Coretta picked up the phone.

"Will you hold one moment, please? Senator Kennedy would like to speak to you."

A voice filled with charm said, "This is John Kennedy. I was just thinking about you and Dr. King. I wanted to express to you my concern about your husband and ask if there is anything I can do."

Kennedy was calling from the lounge of O'Hare Airport in Chicago. There had been much argument among his staff as to whether he should make this call, which would have historic reverberations.

No one was sure of his motivation, perhaps not even himself.

"I appreciate your concern," said Coretta. "I would appreciate anything you can do to help."

"I've spoken to the authorities at Riedsville," Kennedy said. "My brother has spoken to Judge Mitchell."

"Thank you," Coretta said.

Senator Kennedy said with great warmth, "I understand you're expecting a baby."

"Yes."

"I hope you won't let this disturb you too much," Kennedy said. "If there's anything further I can do, please feel free to call me. My secretary will call and give you a number where you can reach me."

"Thank you," said Coretta.

13

Because he bore the name of Martin Luther King III, Marty would grow up with a tremendous privilege and a tremendous responsibility. He would be told over and over again what a great man his father was. And part of the tragedy of his life is that he has never remembered his father as well as he would like to.

Marty stood with his mother, sister, and grandparents, waiting for the SCLC-chartered plane that was bringing King from Riedsville to come to a stop in the private section of the Atlanta airport. Marty was used to being told that his father had gone to jail, and he was used to seeing his father get off airplanes. So Marty thought that his father had gone to jail on the airplane. He was fascinated by the idea.

When King walked down the airplane's steps, Marty was the first to reach him. King was delighted, thinking that his son had outrun the others because he missed his father so much. But Marty ran right past him and up the steps into the airplane, eager to see what was inside. King laughed.

"I got a satchel full of votes," said King Senior to Stanley Levison as he watched King embrace

Coretta and Yolanda. "And I'm going to drop them in the lap of JFK."

"I wouldn't be too much in a hurry to do that," said Levison. He did not want to dampen the spirits of the homecoming, but felt it necessary to be realistic nevertheless. "Kennedy's running a very tight election with Nixon, and he needs that black vote. There are times when the morally wise is also the politically expedient."

Andrew Young was to become one of the most important black men in American history. In 1961 he was part of the Freedom Riders. He would train young people, black and white, in how to deal with being assaulted, because in 1961 the law of the land was that all interstate travel facilities were to be integrated, and blacks and whites trained in nonviolence were boarding buses, determined to see that the law was enforced.

"What if we get arrested?" asked Edwards, a young white man, at one of Young's workshops in Atlanta.

"Don't get out and argue with the cops and say, 'I know my rights,' " said Andy. "That's likely to get you a club on the head. There ain't no point in standing there trying to teach them some constitutional law. Go to jail and wait for your lawyer."

"Supposing they hit us?" asked Ruth, a young black girl.

"To protect your skull," said Andy, demonstrating, "fold your hands over your head. To prevent disfigurement of the face, bring the elbows together in front of the eyes. For girls, to prevent internal injury from kicks, lie on the side and bring the

112

knees upward to the chin; for boys, kneel down and arch over, with skull and face protected."

A few days later Edwards, Ruth and the others were on a Freedom Bus, waving goodbye to Atlanta. Andy watched the bus pull away.

He knew they had to go. Someone had to go. He had gone himself, so he knew what it was like. And now he was the one who had to teach them and send them off. But he knew they would catch hell. He knew they would never be the same after this trip.

He walked for miles after they were gone, and cried.

On an interstate bus approaching Montgomery, Alabama, from the north, a group of Freedom Riders, young blacks and whites in their twenties, were stretching, unkinking their muscles, looking forward to a respite from the cramped quarters when they reached the depot. A young black couple, Ruth and Al, sat talking quietly with John Siegenthaler, from the Attorney General's office. Ruth and Al were concerned about the reception the Freedom Riders might get when they reached Montgomery. Siegenthaler reassured them; he was relatively confident that there would be no trouble.

As the bus pulled into the station a short while later, its passengers noticed that there seemed to be an unusual number of people standing about on the platform, and that most of them were men. The Freedom Riders were surprised, too, to see a number of television cameras. Their apprehension growing, they scanned the gathering. The men in the crowd were staring at the bus, but it was impossible to read their mood from the benign expressions on their faces.

"What do we do?" Ruth asked Siegenthaler as the bus came to a halt.

"We get out," he replied calmly, rising and moving toward the front.

Ruth and Al trailed after him.

At the door, Siegenthaler addressed the driver. "Open it."

The bus door wheezed open, and Siegenthaler stepped down. Turning, he offered a hand to Ruth. She stepped down, followed by Al; then the others began emerging. At the same time, the crowd of men on the platform began edging in, tightening their circle around the bus.

Siegenthaler spoke to one of the men, loudly enough for the others to hear. "I'm John Siegenthaler. Attorney General Robert Kennedy sent me down here to be sure that—"

The man's expression suddenly became mean. Indicating Siegenthaler, he shouted, "Hit that nigger turned inside out!"

A fist slammed into Siegenthaler's face.

The mob erupted in curses and cries of hate, attacking the Freedom Riders.

A mountain of a man slapped Ruth across the face, knocking her to the ground.

A television cameraman, stunned by what he had seen in his camera, cried out at the man who had hit Ruth, "What are you doing! She's a woman!"

The man turned at the sound of his voice. Close by, two men shoved in beside the camera and pushed it off balance. It crashed on the blacktop.

From all sides the men in the crowd attacked the television equipment, smashing the cameras. There were explosions as the television light shattered.

Everywhere Freedom Riders were on the ground, being kicked and hammered with fists, shrieking with terror. Their faces ran with blood.

A group of men dragged Al away from the others and sloshed him with kerosene. One of the men struck a match. Al's clothing burst into flame. Burning, beating at the fire, he screamed for help. For a moment he was a living torch. Then the Freedom Riders were dragging him to the ground, covering him with their bodies, smothering the flames.

The burning, apparently, was too much even for the attackers. They began slipping away, disappearing beyond the circle of people who were mere bystanders. In the middle of the circle, the young people lay sprawled, weeping, battered, moaning. John Siegenthaler, holding his head, peered about at the ring of cold-eyed onlookers. There was not a police officer in sight.

14

In many black houses in the South and North there were pictures of the Kennedy brothers and King together. The origin of their relationship was stormy.

In the aftermath of the brutality at the bus station in Montgomery, the black leaders were called to Washington. King and Ralph Abernathy were summoned, along with Roy Seeger, the tall, austere, soft-spoken head of a national civil rights organization, and Paul Harrison, a union leader who was in the forefront of the battle for black rights.

In the Oval Office, the group met with President Kennedy and his brother Robert, the Attorney General. Also present was a man named Beamer, one of the President's closest high-level aides.

"We want you to stop these Freedom Rides," Robert Kennedy said bluntly to King.

"I don't have the power to stop them," King replied. "And I'm not sure I want to," he added.

"Let's put this in perspective," Beamer said, his manner conciliatory. "You have a friend in this administration," he told the black leaders.

"We're not so sure of that," Harrison said.

Beamer seemed surprised. "Can you explain that, please?"

"There was a plank in the administration's platform," Harrison said, "that pledged a 'sweeping and historical' fight for integration. You pledged you'd wipe out housing discrimination with a stroke of the pen."

"We've appointed Negroes to some very significant jobs," Beamer countered.

"Yes," Seeger said, "and you've appointed three of the most outspoken segregationists to the first three open federal judgeships."

The President raised a hand to stop the debate, then spoke directly to King. "As you may have noticed," he said, "I didn't win the election by the greatest of mandates. The extent of what I can do is somewhat limited."

It was Harrison who responded. "You can take the mandate," he said heatedly. "You're President of the United States. You can do anything you want to do."

The President answered with equal ferocity, "There are other things I want to accomplish in this administration, Mr. Harrison!"

"There is nothing more important than *this* issue," Harrison maintained. "It's the central moral issue in the United States, *and you know it!*"

"But civil rights isn't very good politics, is it?" Roy Seeger said bitterly.

"It's lousy politics," Robert Kennedy admitted.

"I've been in this office many times," Harrison said quietly, with deep feeling. He nodded toward the President. "I've talked to many men in that chair. The best of them was Roosevelt—and I had to threaten a mass march to the Capitol before he would issue decrees that prohibited job discrimination in the war industries on the basis of color." He shook his head sadly. "Just so he would do that . . ."

"That's all very well," Robert Kennedy said crisply. "But I'm the Attorney General of the United States. And right now—at this moment— there is a group of your Freedom Riders surrounded in a church in Montgomery by a mob that wants to kill them. How do I get them out of there?"

Harrison looked at him levelly. "Let them kill them," he said.

Startled, Kennedy flinched.

"Let them kill them," Harrison repeated. "Churches have been bombed. A minister has been beaten to death because he wanted to support black people. Children have been on the verge of starvation. Who ever cared? What do you give a damn about those people in that church for? Because there are newspaper stories being written about them?"

"You make these charges," Robert Kennedy snapped, "but where is the proof? Get the proof for us, then we'll prosecute. We *can't* prosecute without the proof!"

"The FBI gets proof every day!" Harrison countered. "Beatings, rapes, and, yes, murders. The FBI has the proof. But those reports are suppressed or destroyed. There hasn't been *one* conviction!"

This time there was no response from the Attorney General.

Harrison pressed his advantage. "You won't look into that, will you? And I'll tell you why. Because this administration"—he looked directly at the President—"doesn't want a confrontation with J. Edgar Hoover."

Robert Kennedy looked at Harrison, then at King. Conflicting emotions possessed him. He did not know very much about blacks and their problems, but thought of himself as enlightened. Then why did he resent their speaking in this direct manner? And why did he feel that Harrison had struck a true chord in attacking him for his cowardice in dealing with J. Edgar Hoover? Kennedy was usually quick with a deprecating smile. But this time, he couldn't quite manage it.

King emerged from the Oval Office and found Stanley Levison and Damon Lockwood waiting for him.

"How did it go?" asked Levison.

"The New Frontier is not new enough," King replied dryly. "And the Frontier is set too close to the rear." He motioned, leading the way toward the exit.

"Where are you going?" Lockwood wanted to know.

"To Montgomery."

People thought King was never frightened. Bernard Lee knew better, and he became acutely aware of this during the flight to Montgomery.

Bernard was sipping on a Coke when King suddenly began hiccupping.

"What's the matter, Doc, have the hiccups?" Bernard laughed.

King nodded, and Bernard laughed again; the hiccups seemed amusing. But they became more ferocious, and Bernard stood up, alarmed. King's whole body had begun to buck violently.

Bernard ran to the front of the plane and returned with a paper cup full of water. But the hiccups shook King so fiercely that he could not even hold the cup.

"I'd better see if the stewardess can do something," Bernard said, his concern increasing.

King shook his head. He spoke between spasms. "No . . . I'll be all . . . right. . ." But he gasped for air and unbuttoned the top button of his shirt so fiercely that it ripped off.

By the time the plane reached its destination, the hiccups had diminished somewhat, but they had left King weak. Andy Young, meeting them at the airport, was alarmed at his friend's appearance. When he learned the reason for King's exhaustion, he wanted to take him straight to a doctor. But King rejected the idea.

"I'll be all right," he insisted once more.

There was little conversation on the drive into town, and what there was was punctuated by King's continuing hiccups. As the car approached the mob of vengeful whites surrounding the church, the spasms increased in severity again.

"Let's get out of here!" Lee said sharply. "He's got to get to a doctor!"

"No!" King said.

The car stopped at the edge of the mob. Lee got out first, then opened the rear door. King looked out at the faces of the whites, contorted with hate. He hiccupped. Then, drawing on that inner strength that he always summoned up in times of crisis, he steadied himself and got out of the car.

A man in the crowd shouted, "There he is—King!"

There were a few isolated jeers. In general, though, the reaction of the whites was subdued.

121

As King, followed by Lee, Abernathy, Lockwood, and Young, walked casually toward the church, the majority of the whites merely stared at him. It was as if they were finding it impossible to believe that this rather small, chubby black man who was walking among them was really Martin Luther King, fierce crusader of exalted reputation.

When King reached the church steps a white man was standing in the way.

"Excuse me," King said mildly.

The man blinked, looking confused, then stepped aside.

King moved on, entering the church, trailed by his associates.

Outside, the mob recovered. As King and the others proceeded up the aisle toward a platform, the shouts of hate could be heard again, coming from beyond the entrance.

From the platform, King faced the Freedom Riders—young people, black and white—who were managing to look both frightened and defiant at the same time. Scanning the countenances of the young people, he smiled affectionately and encouragingly—and did not hiccup. His affliction had been cured by the intensity of the moment . . . and by his will to meet it.

"You are brave people," he told them.

They seemed to relax a bit.

"We keep hearing," he went on, "that morals can't be legislated. All right. But behavior can be legislated. The law may not be able to make a man love me. But it can keep him from lynching me."

There was a murmur of agreement from the Freedom Riders.

From beyond the walls of the church came a shout. "Come on out! We want to integrate, too!" The voice, a man's, was thick with the venom of hate.

Other shouts overlapped, their words garbled.

Above them a woman shrilled, "If you don't come out, we'll come in and get you!"

The crowd noise rose in volume. "You can't stay in there all night!" someone yelled through the door.

There was a crash. A rock had shattered a window, spraying the assembly with splinters of broken glass.

King raised his arms. "We shall overcome!" he told the Freedom Riders.

They rose and, linking hands, sang robustly:

"We shall overcome,
We shall overcome,
We shall overcome some day.
Oh, deep in my heart I do believe
That we shall overcome some day.

"We are not afraid,
We are not afraid,
We are not afraid today.
Oh, deep in my heart I do believe
That we shall overcome some day."

From Washington, Attorney General Kennedy telephoned Governor Patterson of Alabama. Kennedy's tone was sharp, cutting.

"I'm holding you responsible for the safety of every person in that church," he said.

Patterson was uneasy. "We're doing everything we can," he protested. "But the general can't guarantee the safety of Martin Luther King."

"I want him to say that to me," Kennedy snapped. "I want to hear a general of the United States Army tell me that he can't protect Martin Luther King."

Patterson cleared his throat. "He didn't say it, actually," he said, and paused. "I said it."

Disgusted, Kennedy said, "I see. *You* said it."

The Attorney General hung up and turned to a tall, spare-framed man who had been listening to the conversation with the Governor on another phone. The tall man was Ramsey Clark, Kennedy's deputy. "I want every federal marshal in Alabama in Montgomery," the Attorney General told Clark. "Clear out that mob."

The captives in the church heard their rescuers arriving before they actually saw them. The low rumble seemed to shake the ground. Then one of the Freedom Riders, looking through a broken window, saw the first truck emerge from a side street and turn the corner, and recognized its drab brown color.

"It's the Army—the National Guard!" he called out.

A group crowded around him at the window. As they watched, other trucks pulled up. Guardsmen, armed with rifles, jumped down from the backs of trucks and formed ranks. Isolated jeers greeted them, but the mob of whites was already backing away, retreating into the street. The Guard officers ordered their men to form a line, and the line began slowly advancing on the crowd, forcing it farther back. The whites began drifting away.

The church door opened and a Guard officer appeared. He spoke to the Freedom Riders, giving them the all clear, and they began filing out.

King and Lee rose and walked toward the doorway. They were the last to leave the church. When they stepped outside, they could see that the Freedom Riders were being escorted to cars, then driven away. Most of the whites who had made up the mob had already gone. Satisfied with the outcome, King and Lee moved on, descending the steps of the church.

As they reached the pavement, there was a tinny, rattling sound. A metal object about the size of a tin can had dropped onto the sidewalk in front of the church, seemingly coming from nowhere. King peered at it curiously. But Lee, with a cry of alarm, lunged forward and snatched up the object and hurled it high into the air, over the heads of the Guardsmen. It sailed across the street and landed in an empty parking lot.

There was an explosion.

"A bomb!" King said, astounded. "It was a bomb!"

Guardsmen were racing toward the parking lot.

Lee grabbed King by the arm and hustled him toward the car, where Andy Young and the others were waiting.

15

Home at last.

Wearily, King went up the walk to the house on Sunset Avenue in Atlanta and let himself in—and abruptly halted to look about in wonder. In his absence a major transformation had taken place. The walls had been painted. Curtains had been hung. Respectable furnishings had been brought in. Green, healthy-looking plants were everywhere. The pleasantness was appalling.

Coretta appeared from the kitchen. Beaming, she started toward her husband, then stopped suddenly, perplexed by his expression of dismay.

"What have you done here?" King demanded. "What's happened to my house?"

"Don't you like it?" she asked, her puzzlement compounded. "I've been working so hard on it."

He glared at her, then strode past her, making for the stairs, which he climbed two at a time.

"Martin!" Coretta cried, hurrying after him.

She found him in the bedroom. He was lying on the bed, fully dressed, his shoes on the spread.

"What is the matter with you?" she demanded.

"I don't need this," he said, looking at the ceiling. "I picked this house because it was the poorest place I could find near the church."

With effort, Coretta kept her temper under control. "I wanted some place nice for you to come back to after all the terrible things you go to," she said.

"I don't want it," he retorted angrily. "You and the children can live in it. I don't want it."

Coretta moved on into the room, stopping at the foot of the bed. "Now, you listen to me, you," she said determinedly. "For the first time in our lives, we're going to have a real home. Yes, and it's going to have drapes and slipcovers. And we're going to have family dinners—just you and me and the children. And we're not going to talk about the terrible things that are happening to you on the road and in jail. It's going to be a nice place for you to come back to and look forward to—a place that will always be here!"

King was staring at her in astonishment, startled by her ferocity.

"And get your shoes off the bed!" Coretta snapped.

King broke into a wide grin. The grin exploded, becoming a sunburst of hilarious laughter. Holding his middle, the stoic man of principle rocked from side to side on the bed, howling with glee.

Watching him, Coretta scowled crossly at first, thinking that he was making fun of her. Then gradually she began to smile, realization dawning: He was laughing so boisterously for the simple reason that—for this moment, at least—he was happy.

He reached out to her, and she sat on the edge of the bed.

Then Coretta was laughing too, at herself. The two of them had a tremendous humor. It was the saving of them, and it was one of the reasons that they loved each other.

It was early morning. At the office of the Southern Christian Leadership Conference, King, Lockwood, McKeecham, and Levison were seated at a small table, talking quietly, making plans for a later meeting in another state. At this early hour they were the only ones present in the office. Then the outer door opened, the click of the latch disturbing the quiet, and Andy Young entered. He moved sluggishly, and his face was drawn. He looked as if he had not had any sleep in a long while.

"What is it?" King asked him, as he sat down heavily in the extra chair.

"They found those boys—Goodman, Schwerner, and Chaney," he said, his voice choked with emotion.

King, with so much on his mind, had to think for a moment. Then, remembering: "Those kids in Philadelphia, Mississippi?"

Young nodded. "The two white boys and the black. They were helping us."

"Dead . . ." Damon Lockwood guessed.

Young nodded again. "They found the bodies buried in a dam."

"How did it happen?" asked Lockwood.

"Nobody knows yet," Young said wearily. "They spent a night in jail. They were released in the morning. Nobody's seen them since—till now."

"Two of them white . . ." King mused. "I wonder how some of our people who are saying that whites shouldn't be part of the movement are feeling now." He looked at Andy Young again. "Who did it?"

"Some of the men in the sheriff's office go around bragging that they were the ones who put the bullets into Goodman."

"We're going to Philadelphia, Mississippi," King announced.

McKeecham stared at him. "Are you serious?"

"They'll kill you," Lockwood said without conviction. Cautioning King was like trying to talk a hurricane out of its path. "They'll tear you apart."

King addressed Andy Young again. "Contact the FBI. Tell them we're coming. Tell them we'll need protection."

"What do you think the FBI consists of in Philadelphia, Mississippi?" Young snorted. "They're Mississippi boys. They probably have lunch and dinner with the murderers. They're part of the community. They don't want to rock the boat. The only people relevant to them are the local white people."

Levison leaned forward at the table. "Martin, we have that fund-raising next week," he reminded his friend. "It's important."

King shook his head. "No, nothing is more important than going to Philadelphia, Mississippi," he said. "Nothing."

Accompanied by several other members of the SCLC, King departed for Mississippi the next day, traveling by car. When they arrived in the small town of Philadelphia, they met with the local leaders of the movement and were joined by civil rights activists from other parts of the country who had been drawn to Philadelphia by the horror of the crime against Goodman, Schwerner, and Chaney. With Rabbi Weiss from New York, they planned a memorial service for the three young victims, to be held on the steps of the courthouse.

There was a large crowd for the service, but only a small fraction of the congregation were mourners. The others were local whites who had come to show their hatred. Among them were the sheriff, Rainey, and his deputy, Price—big men, with their bellies bulging over their gun belts. Listening to the rabbi conducting the service, they smirked, laughed, and winked.

"I wish every racist, black and otherwise," Rabbi Weiss said, speaking from the steps, "could be with us today to say thank you to three boys who died."

The whites muttered belligerently.

"Two white and one black," Rabbi Weiss continued. "They went beyond the color of their skin. They believed that we are all part of a whole. They believed that people of all races can live together."

There were shouts of derision from the whites, loud and threatening.

Andy Young, standing to the left of King, leaned forward slightly and spoke to Ralph Abernathy, who flanked King to the right. "I think it's time for a prayer," he said.

Abernathy scowled at him. "Whenever we're in trouble, you always call on me to say a prayer."

"And make it a quick one," Young advised.

"You don't mind if I keep my eyes open, do you?" Abernathy returned.

Young ascended the steps, joining the rabbi. "Dr. Abernathy," he announced, "will now deliver a prayer."

As Abernathy climbed the steps, Young and the rabbi descended.

Abernathy raised his eyes heavenward. "Look down on us, oh Lord, and forgive us poor sinners," he intoned. "For we all must be forgiven. Who knows?" he said, his eyes scanning the crowd. "Perhaps the murderers of Goodman, Schwerner, and Chaney are near us at this moment."

"You're damn right," a heckler taunted from the crowd. "They're right here."

Now the threats were being shouted again.

Abernathy glanced quickly at Young, then abruptly brought the prayer—and the service—to an end. "Amen!" he said with exaggerated finality, hurrying down the steps.

"Let's go!" Young declared.

He and Abernathy led the way, moving quickly along the line of jeering whites. King and Bernard Lee followed at their heels.

"Where's that King nigger?" a sharp-faced white man sneered. "I thought he was coming down here!"

King hesitated, staring at the man.

Bernard Lee urged him on. "Keep walking, Doc!" he said anxiously.

As they proceeded, the man's shout pursued them. "Where's the coon? Where's Martin Luther Coon? Why don't he come out here?"

King slowed his pace.

"They don't know you're here," Bernard Lee warned. "Don't do anything."

Andy Young and Ralph Abernathy were now far ahead.

"Where's the little coward?" the white man snarled.

King turned and started back.

Bernard Lee grabbed him by an arm, holding him. "Where you going, Doc?"

King did not answer. He pulled free of Lee's hold and turned back toward where the heckler was standing.

Running, Bernard Lee caught up to him and stopped him once more. "What are you doing?" he demanded, frightened.

"Let me go!" King ordered, trying to yank loose from Lee's grip. "That man wants to talk to me! I want to talk to him!"

"Don't pay any attention to that trash!"

"I'm going over there!" King insisted. "If they want me, they can take me!"

"That's exactly what they want you to do."

Bernard looked around wildly for Andy and Abernathy, but they were almost out of sight. He turned to a tall, heavy, middle-aged black man close by. "Sir! Sir! This is Dr. Martin Luther King, Jr.! I don't want anything to happen to him!"

Bernard and the man ran to King, who had begun making his way back to the mob. They had difficulty holding onto him. It was almost as though there were a death wish in King, as though he would rather be destroyed than live in a world like this.

"Let me go!" he shouted.

"No! No!" said Bernard.

He and the middle-aged man dragged King away.

Back in Atlanta, King was haunted by the memory of having been drummed out of Philadelphia in humiliation when all he had wanted to do was give a memorial service for three dead boys.

In his office, he began to dictate to his secretary. "There are beatings, rapes and murders taking place every day in the South. They are being reported to the FBI. The problem is that too many of the agents of the FBI in the Southern states share the racist attitudes of the law enforcement officials there."

Damon Lockwood looked at him, appalled. "Martin!"

King continued. "They're more interested in keeping their relationships with the local police and people who are promoting segregation than to see that people are protected."

"Martin," said Damon in alarm, "you can't give out a statement like that. You don't realize how defensive Hoover is about criticism of the FBI. You can't fight with Hoover! Presidents have been afraid to do it."

Damon picked up the pad on which the secretary had taken down King's words and was about to crumple the paper.

King wrested the paper from Damon's clenched fist.

"You can go," Damon said to the secretary.

"No. Stay," said King.

He flattened out the crumpled paper and turned to the secretary again. "The FBI is most effective as an agency for the solution of ordinary crimes, and perhaps it should stick to that."

Inside J. Edgar Hoover's office, a group of newswomen had gathered. They were discussing something else when Hoover said suddenly, irrelevantly, "Martin Luther King is the most notorious liar in the United States."

Clyde Tolson and William Sullivan, standing behind Hoover, were stunned. Then Tolson scribbled something quickly and handed the note to Hoover. Hoover looked at him with a bit of a smile. "Mr. Tolson has handed me this note, and tells me I should keep these statements concerning King off the record, but that's none of his business."

Tolson turned pale.

Sullivan looked at Hoover warily.

Hoover continued. "I made it for the record, and you can use it for the record. Have you taken it down word for word? Martin Luther King is the most notorious liar in the United States."

16

In the spring of 1963, King flew to Birmingham. The Reverend Fred Shuttlesworth drove King, Andy Young, Stanley Levison and Damon Lockwood about the city. Fred Shuttlesworth was a man of extraordinary courage. He had been bombed and beaten, but he continued to stand with incredible bravery against the forces of the most violent city in the South—Birmingham, Alabama.

"Toughest city this side of Johannesburg, South Africa," Shuttlesworth said.

"That's why we're here," King said.

Shuttlesworth drove to the town's main business section. Reaching it, he suddenly pulled into a parking space. Keeping the motor running, he pointed to a man who was standing on the other side of the street, talking to a policeman.

"That's him—Bull Connor," Reverend Shuttlesworth said.

The man he was indicating appeared to be in his sixties. But he was burly, thick-chested, thick-limbed, built somewhat on the order of a beer barrel. He was wearing dark glasses, and his gun was slung low on his hip. He was a living caricature of a Southern redneck turned lawman.

"Nobody looks like that," Damon Lockwood said. "They must have made him up."

Shuttlesworth was not amused. "Bull Connor *is* Birmingham," he said.

"What's his background?" Andy Young wanted to know.

"He was a sports announcer," said their guide. "Very popular man. Then he got it into his mind to go into politics."

"I know Mr. Connor!" Levison suddenly exclaimed. "I thought that big belly was familiar. I remember him from my union days. He was a first class strikebreaker. He had an organization that kidnapped organizers from their homes—beat them up, dumped them on the side of the road . . . killed some of them."

The Reverend Fred Shuttlesworth turned to King. "Still think you can desegregate this place nonviolently?"

"If you can desegregate Birmingham, you can desegregate the South," Damon said.

"There is a medium called television," said King. "It captures faces. We're going to use it to make people aware of what we've known all our lives. Television is the medium through which we're going to bring this country face to face with itself."

Shortly afterward, King entered the study of the church where his brother, A. D., was pastor. A. D. was seated behind his desk.

"You were supposed to meet me at the airport," King said. He spoke casually, without intimation of reprimand.

A. D. looked at him apprehensively, as if expecting a scolding.

King put his briefcase down on the desk, then settled in a side chair. "I'll be talking here tonight, you know," he said to his brother. "I want you to give me one of your special introductions."

A. D. lowered his eyes. "I can't do it, Martin," he said miserably. "I'm not up to it."

King acted surprised. "What do you mean, you're not up to it? You're a great speaker." He laughed affectionately. "You're lovable, A. D. That's what you are—you're lovable. You know why?" he said, suddenly looking thoughtful. "Because you make people feel important."

Tears brimmed in A. D.'s eyes. "They're asking me to resign."

"Nobody's going to ask you to resign," said King, "because you're going to be brilliant tonight."

There was standing room only that night in the church for King's appearance. For the most part the audience was made up of blacks, but here and there a white face could be seen.

Reaching the pulpit, A. D. cleared his throat and looked about expectantly. The audience became quiet.

"Martin Luther King has become a famous man," A. D. said, beginning the introduction. "But to me he's still my brother."

There were soft whisperings, now that the man in the pulpit had identified himself.

Martin and A. D. had been talking all day, until just a few minutes before the meeting, and Martin had made him feel calm and sure of himself.

"I opened one of the letters that came to our house," A. D. continued. "It said, 'This isn't a threat,

139

but a promise—your head will be blown off as sure as Christ made little green apples.' "

There were murmurs of indignation.

"But my brother has a hard head," A. D. said, smiling, relieving the audience's sudden tension. "I remember one day he was leaning against an upstairs banister. He went over head first. It must have been twenty feet from the top of the stairs to the floor. Landed right on his head." He shrugged. "Nothing broken. Nothing scratched."

There were a few chuckles.

"Then, one day he was riding a bike. A car hit the bike—and my brother hit the sidewalk. Right over the handlebars. Hit the cement. Still okay. Not even dented."

There was some laughter now.

A. D. warmed to his subject. "There was the time we were playing baseball. My brother was the catcher. I was up to bat. I took a swing, the bat slipped. Hit him right in the head. Knocked him flat. I bent over him. 'You all right?' I asked. He opened his eyes and he said, 'You're out! You missed on that third strike!' "

The laughter was loud and enthusiastic this time.

"One time," he said, his manner sobering, "I told all that to one of the women in a congregation, and she said to me, 'The Lord had a hand on him even then. He was saving him for us. No harm could come to him.' And I think maybe she was right. I think maybe He gave my brother a hard head for that purpose." Turning, he gestured toward the wings. "My brother . . . Martin Luther King, Jr. . . . ."

King appeared and crossed to the pulpit.

The applause was a roar, swelling, pressing outward against the walls of the church.

A. D. stepped back from the pulpit, and his brother took his place. Smiling, King raised his hands in response to the ovation, then began gesturing for quiet. Gradually, the applause subsided.

"Thank you," King said. He glanced in his brother's direction. "I always thought A. D. was a better preacher than I am," he said, "and tonight proves it."

The mild laughter was appreciative.

"Tonight," King told the audience, "many people—including black people—are asking why we are in Birmingham. Why direct action? Why sitins, marches, and so forth? My friends," he said, answering the question, "we have not made a single gain in civil rights without determined legal and nonviolent pressure. It is lamentable, but it is an historical fact that privileged groups seldom give up their privileges voluntarily."

There were outcries of agreement.

As King started to speak again, a white man in the front row rose and walked toward the pulpit. King peered at him curiously. There was nothing threatening about the man's manner. King guessed that the white man intended to say something in support of his statement or his presence in Birmingham.

Suddenly—too late to draw back—King saw the malice in the man's eyes. The incident in the Harlem shoe store, when he had been stabbed, flashed across his mind. Then the man lunged, hitting him with his fist. King was knocked backwards, momentarily off balance. A cry of alarm rose from the audience. The white man struck him again.

Then Bernard Lee had hold of the attacker and was grappling with him, pinning his arms behind his back. Blacks, pushing forward from the audience, reached out to grab the man. There were loud cries of rage. The expression on the white man's face had changed considerably. Where there had been bravado and hate there was now terror.

"Take him out!" King ordered Lee. "Don't let anybody near him!"

But Lee and the assailant were surrounded now. Angry fists were being shaken in the white man's face. The entire audience seemed to be demanding revenge.

"Stop! Leave him alone!" King called out.

For a moment they seemed to hold back. Taking advantage of the brief hesitation, King moved to where Bernard Lee was holding his prisoner and put a protective arm around the cowed and terrified man.

"What would you like to do?" King asked the audience. "Kill him?"

They fell silent, subdued.

"That isn't our movement!" King told them. "Would you like to use Molotov cocktails? That is not our movement!"

Sheepishly, those who had surrounded Bernard Lee and the white man were backing away.

"I'll tell you what our movement is," King said. "It's to understand him," he said, indicating the white man. "Yes, even him! It's to ask what it would be like if you were taught since you were a child

. . . since you were baby enough to crawl . . . that the Negro is a *thing!*"

Those who had mounted the pulpit were now retreating to their seats.

"If you were taught from your parents," King went on, "from your teachers, from even your ministers and the people sitting next to you in church that it isn't wrong to hate, what would you be then?"

There were murmurs of agreement, understanding. Bernard Lee was leading the white man away.

"That's what this movement is," King told them. "It's to reveal these people to themselves."

17

There were close to three dozen of them. Headed by the Reverend Fred Shuttlesworth, they were marching silently, single file, up one of Birmingham's main streets. Some of them carried placards: *Equal Opportunity And Human Dignity. Birmingham Merchants Unfair. Don't Buy Segregation. Khrushchev Could Eat Here—Why Not American Negroes?* From all sides came the jeers of white bystanders. The black marchers, men and women, kept their heads high, eyes forward.

At a corner, Bull Connor, in charge of public safety, stood waiting. Bull's jaw was set, his eyes concealed behind dark glasses. To one side of him stood a squad of policemen, commanded by an aide, a lieutenant named Dunne. At Connor's other side was the pack of police dogs, snarling, restrained by special handlers. Behind him stood a police van and a group of firemen, their hoses at the ready.

When the marchers were approximately a half-block away, Bull Connor motioned to Lieutenant Dunne, who in turn signaled to his men. The police officers deployed, becoming a barrier in the way of the marchers. A few yards short of the line of policemen, Shuttlesworth raised a hand and stopped. The marchers closed ranks behind him.

"Take down their names," Bull Connor commanded the lieutenant.

"Back up against the wall there!" Dunne bellowed to the marchers. "I want your names!"

The marchers obeyed quietly.

"What's your name?" the lieutenant asked the leader of the marchers.

"Reverend Fred Shuttlesworth."

Bull Connor stepped forward. "So you're that nigger Shuttlesworth, are you?" he said.

"Yes, sir."

"Shuttlesworth, you've done more to hurt the niggers in Birmingham, to set them back, than any man in the history of the city," Bull sneered.

The Reverend smiled. "It all depends on how you look at it, Mr. Connor."

"You're going to find that I'm your best friend," he announced.

Shuttlesworth peered at him in amazement. "You're my best friend, Mr. Connor? That's a surprise."

Bull Connor pulled what looked like a legal document from his hip pocket. "I have an injunction here from Judge Jenkins banning all demonstrations. I'm asking you to disband."

"We can't do that," said Shuttlesworth.

Bull shrugged. "Get the wagon!" he ordered.

The lieutenant turned and gestured, and the police van began moving up.

The marchers waited stoically.

146

They were no longer Bull Connor's concern. He addressed the firemen and the men who were handling the dogs. "We won't need those—yet," he told them. He seemed disappointed.

In the room in the Gaston Motel in Birmingham that had become his headquarters, King was conferring with Andy Young on tactics for the next day's march. When the phone rang, Young picked up the receiver. He identified himself, listened for a second, then handed the phone to King.

"It's Washington—the Attorney General," he said.

Robert Kennedy was calling from the Oval Office. With him was his brother, the President.

"This is going to destroy everything we've been fighting for," the Attorney General said. "Birmingham is the wrong place."

"We have to go ahead," King said firmly.

"It isn't the time!" Kennedy protested.

King said quietly, "It's never the time."

Kennedy was conciliatory, attempting to smooth the way to compromise. "If you wait a few months—"

"We've waited long enough," King interrupted. "We can't stop now."

In disgust, Robert Kennedy hung up the phone. Turning to his brother, he said, "He won't stop. What do we do?"

The President smiled faintly. "Can you imagine the balls it takes to try to integrate Birmingham?"

The Attorney General was grim. "But what are we going to do?"

The President gave the question a moment of

147

thought. "The same thing we always do," he said at last. "Nothing."

At the headquarters in the Gaston Motel, the Reverend Fred Shuttlesworth, out on bail, knocked on the door and opened it simultaneously. He was followed into the room by a trio of other clergymen.

The four crossed to where King was going over some papers with Andy Young. King looked up.

"Some people to see you," Shuttlesworth said. He introduced the three clergymen, all white: Father Mikeljohn, Reverend Redding, Rabbi Kaplan.

"Are you gentlemen joining us?" King asked hopefully.

"We're here to talk," Father Mikeljohn replied. "I understand you're going to use children in your protests."

King nodded. "Yes, that's right."

"It hardly seems brave to send children to do a man's work," said Mikeljohn.

"Children are very useful," Andy Young interjected. "They can't be pressured to stop demonstrating because they might lose their jobs."

"We want you to leave Birmingham," Rabbi Kaplan said sharply. "We're able to deal with our own problems."

"You haven't dealt with them very well up to this time."

Ignoring Young, Reverend Redding told King, "We're not the only ones who want you to leave. There are black people in this community who feel the same way."

"I'll *bet* there are," Young said dryly.

"I can't understand you," King said, disappointed. "You're clergymen."

"We're here because we *are* clergymen," the Reverend Redding responded defensively.

King looked at him steadily, with childlike directness and bewilderment. "How can you stand there in your pulpits and preach to your congregations about Jesus?"

"What you are doing here is illegal!" Rabbi Kaplan said tightly.

King directed his level gaze at him. "Everything Adolf Hitler did in Germany was *legal*," he said. "Yet I know that if I'd lived in Germany at that time, I would have aided the Jews. I would have openly advocated disobeying the law." He turned to the other clergymen. "Where are *your* voices when defiance and hatred are called for by white men who sit in your churches?" He looked away grimly, forcing back the anger that he felt rising in himself.

"Stop these demonstrations!" Reverend Redding pleaded.

"No."

"If you continue, people will be hurt," Redding added. "People may be killed."

"Yes, perhaps," King conceded.

There was a second of silence.

Then Redding spoke again. "You're a man who preaches nonviolence," he said to King, his voice heavy with emotion, "and prays in his heart for violence."

King peered at him searchingly. He was not

really looking at the clergyman, he was looking inside himself, wondering if the Reverend Redding could possibly be right about him. Then, without having fully satisfied himself as to what the truth might be, he turned away. Behind him he could hear Shuttlesworth ushering the visitors from the room. King continued to stare into space, examining the small self-doubt that had been planted in his mind.

Jailing the marchers did not stop the marches. Those who went to jail were replaced by others. The jails filled up. The marches continued. With no places left to imprison the marchers, Bull Connor resorted to the fire hoses. When marchers advanced on the intersection that Connor had chosen to defend, they were met with powerful blasts of water that knocked them to the pavement, slammed them against walls, ripped the clothing from their bodies.

Scattered and driven back one day, the marchers regrouped the next day, with new volunteers replacing the injured, and marched again. Each day they met with the same insurmountable obstacle, fusillade after fusillade from the fire hoses. And each day the result was the same: the marchers retreated in a seeming rout. On the face of it, they were engaging in an exercise of consummate futility.

Other elements were at work, however. The news media were covering the marches. All over the nation, people were seeing the marches on television, reading about them in their papers. Watching the TV screen, Americans coast-to-coast were eyewitnesses to Bull Connor's brutality and the marchers' courage. It was beginning to be said—even in Birmingham—that Bull Connor was the civil rights movement's best ally.

If Bull Connor was aware that, in the classic irony, he was winning the battles and losing the war, he showed no sign of it. Mindlessly, he persisted in bringing out the fire hoses. Then, at exactly the wrong moment—as if driven by a compulsion to destroy himself—he introduced his most savage and inhumane weapon into the conflict—the dogs.

Lieutenant Dunne was the first to see the children among the marchers that day. "Jesus Christ, it's kids!" he exclaimed to Connor, staring in disbelief at the protesters as they approached the intersection.

"Makes no difference," said Connor without emotion, watching the advance.

The children were in the first line of the march, eight-, nine-, and ten-year-olds, walking side by side with their parents. They looked both frightened and indomitable. As they neared the barricade of police officers, firemen, and dogs, Bull Connor stepped forward. The march halted.

Connor confronted a little girl. "What do you want?" he snapped.

She was not able to pronounce the word clearly in such terrifying circumstances. "F'eedom," she answered, drawing closer to her mother, her eyes wide and dark.

"Go back!" Connor commanded.

The marchers stood fast.

"Will you go back?"

Not one marcher moved.

Connor turned his back on them. Retreating to the barricade, he called out to the firemen, "Let 'em go!"

The blasts of water hit the first rank of marchers. The children screamed. A small boy was picked up by a stream of water and washed into the gutter. A girl's blouse tore away. A boy in a striped T-shirt, fleeing, was caught by a blast from a hose and smashed against a storefront window. But the children's determination seemed even more fierce than their parents'. Knocked down, battered, bruised, they picked themselves up and ran back to the front lines—and were blasted off their feet and driven back again.

That plucky defiance and unconquerable resolution triggered a rage in Connor. Watching the teeming street, his eyes strayed to the handlers who were holding the German shepherds. At last he turned, the sunglasses blanking his expression— and gave the signal. The leashes were unsnapped. Teeth bared, the shepherds sprang forward. Suddenly the street was full of dogs, snarling, snapping at children, leaping at the faces of adults. What the fire hoses had failed to do this time, the dogs accomplished. Shrieking in terror, shielding their faces with their arms, the marchers fled.

Bull Connor gloated.

But in retreat the children were victorious. For through the eyes of the television cameras, the nation had watched Connor's savagery. And the nation was appalled.

In their headquarters at the Gaston Motel, King and his associates, watching television, were witnesses to Bull Connor's brutality.

"I'm going out there," King said.

"No!" Young replied instantly. "He won't turn a dog loose on you—he'll put you in jail. Those jails are jammed, but he has room for one more."

But King had made up his mind. "There comes a time when a movement is judged by its leader. I can't stay out of jail while others are in."

"It's too dangerous!" Young insisted.

"Bull Connor owns those jails," Damon Lockwood added unnecessarily. "He can start a riot . . . anything. . . . You could be killed 'by accident.'"

Murmuring agreement, Stanley Levison raised another consideration. "We've run out of bail money," he reminded King. "You're the only one who can help us raise it. If you go to jail, *all* the people will stay in jail—indefinitely."

Abruptly, King got up and left them. The bedroom door closed behind him. The others looked at each other, perplexed, not knowing what to think of his sudden exit. Awaiting his return, they turned their eyes up to the television screen again. At the intersection downtown, a mop-up was in progress. The marchers who had been injured were being carried away. The dogs had been called back and were on their leashes again.

King emerged from the bedroom. It was instantly clear to his associates what decision he had made. He was wearing dungarees, his jail clothes.

"I'm going," he announced. "I don't know what's

153

going to happen in jail—to me or to the others. But"—he glanced toward the TV set—"there are millions of people in this country watching us. I can't stay here, safe. I have to make a commitment."

It was obvious to them that there was no longer any point in trying to talk him out of it.

"Then go," Ralph Abernathy said, getting up and heading toward the bedroom. "But you're not going to jail alone. Give me a minute to get into my jailhouse duds. I'm going with you."

They left the room together a short while later, both wearing dungarees. As they departed, they were followed by the muffled sound of singing coming from the headquarters room:

"We shall overcome
We shall overcome some day.
Oh, deep in my heart I do believe
That we shall overcome some day."

Hearing it, King and Abernathy looked at each other. Both had tears in their eyes—tears brought on by a sudden surge of pride.

From the motel they drove to town, then up the main street. Nearing the intersection where Bull Connor had set up the barricade of policemen, firemen, and dogs, they parked the car and walked on into the melee. Bystanders along the street recognized them. Whites cursed them. Blacks called out encouragement, or sang softly, or knelt and prayed.

When they reached Bull Connor and his men and dogs, the guardian of public safety wasted no words on them.

"Arrest them!" Bull ordered.

Policemen grabbed them, twisted their arms, pushed their heads down, and shoved them roughly into the waiting van.

18

In the King home, Coretta paced the living room, staying near the phone. From upstairs the voices of her children rose in a sudden outbreak of exuberance. She sighed. Being children, they occasionally failed in their effort to be as quiet as possible in deference to her tense mood. She chewed nervously at her lips. Every once in a while she glared at the phone, commanding it to ring. But it would not be intimidated; it remained mute.

There was a knock.

Coretta hurried to the door and opened it to admit her father-in-law.

"Hello," King senior said, looking at her hopefully.

"Hello." She kissed him.

"Hear anything?"

"Nothing," she said.

At that moment, the phone rang.

Coretta ran to it and snatched up the receiver. Robert Kennedy was on the line.

"I know you tried to reach the President," the Attorney General said. "He's not available right now."

"Oh . . ." she said coolly.

"Is there anything I can do for you?"

"My husband is in jail in Birmingham," she stated.

"Yes, I know."

But she did not call the President every time Martin spent a night in jail. "I haven't heard from him in three days," she said, her voice strained. "He always calls me after he's arrested. Even his lawyers can't get in to see him. I don't know what's happened to him."

Kennedy responded sympathetically, "Birmingham is a difficult place. We're trying everything we can. I'll let you know as soon as I hear anything."

It was a dismissal. "Thank you," she said, somewhat bitterly. She doubted he seriously intended to intervene.

She hung up, then told King senior what the Attorney General had said.

"I don't know why you thought you could talk to the President," he replied.

"He told me to call him if I ever needed him."

"That was before the election," King senior scoffed. "He's in now. He don't need us." He looked at his daughter-in-law closely. "You look awful tired."

"I am. I can't sleep, I can't—" She was suddenly thoughtful. "I can't remember when I ate last. I'm hungry."

"You got to keep up your strength," he reproved.

He followed her to the kitchen, where Coretta made herself a sandwich. While she ate, they talked about the situation in Birmingham and their concern for Martin's safety. They had sat for about an hour when they were interrupted by the sound of quarreling from upstairs. Excusing herself, Coretta returned to the living room.

"What's going on up there?" she called up the stairs.

"He's trying to use the telephone," Yolanda answered, referring to her brother, "but there's some woman on it."

"What?" Puzzled, Coretta went to the downstairs phone and picked up the receiver.

"Hello?"

An operator said edgily, "Mrs. King?"

"Yes."

"Will you please get your child off the phone?" the operator said. "The President of the United States is trying to reach you."

Her hand over the mouthpiece, Coretta leaned toward the stairs. "You children! Get away from that phone!"

She heard the click of the upstairs receiver and then John Kennedy's voice.

"Mrs. King? I understand you talked to my brother."

Coretta smiled gratefully. "Yes."

"I'm sorry I couldn't call you personally," the President explained. "I was with my father. He's ill."

So the call from his brother had not been merely a put-off. "I'm sorry," she said, her bitterness draining away.

"About the situation in Birmingham . . . I want you to know that the Justice Department has been sent in. They talked to your husband. He's all right."

Coretta felt a surge of relief. "Is he free?"

"No," Kennedy said. "But we have our people in there. He's safe. You don't have to worry about him."

"Thank God."

The President said gently, "We'll be keeping on top of the situation. If you get worried again, feel free to call the Attorney General or my press secretary, Mr. Salinger. They'll know where to reach me."

"Thank you," she said. "Thank you *very* much."

For a long moment after she had hung up the phone, she stood motionless, her head bowed, her eyes closed. Then, recovering her composure, she walked back to the kitchen to tell her father-in-law what she had learned. King senior looked up as she came in. He had not heard the conversation and did not know who had called, but he did not need to ask what the message had been. That Martin was safe was written in the smoothness of Coretta's face, the relief in her eyes.

It was Easter Sunday—a warm day, bright and sunny. The streets of downtown Birmingham were all but deserted. The only evidence of the troubles was the barricade of policemen, firemen, and dogs at the intersection. Even here, however, there was an indication that the holy day was being observed —the police and firemen were at less than half force.

Approaching this scene of relative tranquillity was a small group of blacks, led by Andy Young. There was no hostility in their manner. It was clear, though, from the way they moved, that they had arrived at this place, at this time, with a particular purpose in mind. Lieutenant Dunne, the man in charge of the barricade at the moment, watched them curiously at first. But as they got closer his curiosity turned to nervousness.

"Hold it!" Dunne said, stepping out to meet the blacks.

They obeyed and stood waiting as he approached.

"You're not allowed to have demonstrations," the lieutenant told them.

Andy Young spoke for the group. "This is Easter Sunday," he said mildly, "and nearly every leader of our Movement is in jail. We want to walk to the jail, kneel, and say a few prayers. Just an Easter Sunday meeting."

Lieutenant Dunne shook his head. "I can't allow you to do that."

"Why?"

"Because it's against the law."

"If you really want to enforce the law," Young replied, "move your men back two blocks and give us a half-hour. But if you want to beat us"—he gestured to those behind him. The adults stepped aside, revealing that they were accompanied by their children—"if you want to beat up children, just like your own kids, go ahead. It's your choice."

Lieutenant Dunne shifted uneasily.

Reverend Fred Shuttlesworth, a step or two behind Andy Young, lowered himself to his knees. Eyes upraised, he sang softly:

"Ain't gonna let nobody turn me around
Turn me around
Turn me around . . ."

"We're not trying to destroy you or fight you," Young explained to the lieutenant. "We're trying to change you because we're going to be living together. And in freeing ourselves we're freeing you, and one day you're going to become aware of it."

Behind him others in the group were kneeling, taking up the song:

> "Ain't gonna let nobody turn me around
> Keep on a-walking
> Keep on a-talking
> Gonna build a brand new world . . ."

Lieutenant Dunne glanced quickly, almost surreptitiously, at his men, then turned his eyes to the kneeling, singing blacks once more. He was undecided, but clearly wavering in favor of the blacks.

Then a police car came rolling up, and Bull Connor came storming out.

"What's going on here!" Connor demanded.

"They just want to go and pray by the jail," Dunne answered defensively.

"Disperse them!" Connor ordered. He motioned to the firemen. "Bring in the hoses! Turn them on!"

Not one of the firemen moved. Staring fascinatedly at the kneeling blacks, they seemed half-mesmerized.

"Hoses!" Connor raised his voice. "Turn on the hoses!"

There was a stirring among the firemen, but no one followed the order.

Reverend Shuttlesworth got to his feet, crossed to the nearest fireman, and planted himself directly in front of the nozzle of the hose the man was holding.

"Go ahead," Shuttlesworth said calmly. "Turn it on."

The fireman backed away a step, wincing, as if he had been told that his hose was a weapon and was suddenly afraid that it might go off accidentally.

"Turn them on!" Bull Connor bellowed.

The firemen remained immobile.

Andy Young stepped forward. He passed between a pair of firemen and walked on. As deliberately, Shuttlesworth followed him. Behind them the other blacks rose from their knees and, still singing softly, began filing through the line of firemen.

"Turn on the hoses!" Bull Connor roared desperately. "Turn them on!"

But the firemen were moving back, making way for the blacks. The hoses hung limply in their hands, like melted lances.

Bull Connor, speechless at last, stared incredulously as the blacks continued to pass through the line. His mouth twitched, as if he were tasting his own bile. Then his shoulders sagged slightly, and he turned to go back to the police car. He no longer strutted as he walked away.

The church was packed when King arrived. Accompanied by Andy Young and Bernard Lee, he entered by the rear door, where he was met by Shuttlesworth and several other leaders of the black protest in Birmingham. They embraced him joyously.

163

"You did it, Martin. You made it possible," Shuttlesworth congratulated him. "You came here with a few hundred people and you raised an army of thousands."

"No, I didn't do it—the people did it," King replied.

"Bull Connor helped," added Andy Young. "Let's not forget that. He turned Birmingham into a battleground. People were afraid to come to town. The department stores were empty. Birmingham was dying. The only way the white establishment could save it was to call off Bull Connor and desegregate."

"Whoever did it—whatever did it—it's done," Reverend Shuttlesworth said exuberantly. "The toughest town in the South has been desegregated."

From the people gathered in the church came calls demanding King.

"They know who did it," Bernard Lee said. "They want you, Martin. Go on out there."

As King appeared in the pulpit there was a roar of applause. He gestured for quiet, but the ovation crescendoed until it seemed to rattle the windows and shake the frame building on its foundation.

At last, after many minutes, King was able to speak. "As you have heard," he said, "we have an agreement. It calls for desegregation of lunch counters, restrooms, fitting rooms, and drinking fountains in planned stages within ninety days after signing."

The applause rose again.

"Listen . . ." King begged.

When they had quieted down, he continued, "It calls for the upgrading and hiring of Negroes on a nondiscriminatory basis throughout the industrial community of Birmingham. And there will be official cooperation with the Movement's legal representatives in working out the release of all jailed persons on bond . . . or on their personal recognizance."

Cheers shook the building again.

"You have overcome!" King concluded.

19

In the office of the Southern Christian Leadership Conference in Atlanta, King and several of his associates were seated at a long table, discussing the Movement's shaky financial condition.

When the phone rang, Bernard Lee answered it. After a moment, he handed the receiver to King. "It's Fred Shuttlesworth," he said.

The conversation lasted for only a minute or so. As King listened, his expression went flat, his eyes glazed. When he hung up, he sat in silence almost as long as the conversation had gone on.

"Martin, what is it?" Stanley Levison finally asked.

"They bombed Reverend Cross's church in Birmingham," King said. "They killed four children . . . four little girls. . . . They were sitting in Sunday school."

The others were speechless, stunned.

King blinked away the mental images. Abruptly he turned to Bernard Lee. "Find out what time the next plane leaves for Birmingham," he said.

Lee picked up the receiver and began dialing.

"Four little children," King said despondently. "What are we doing? Is it worth it? Is *anything* worth that?" He lowered his head, covering his eyes. "Am I a monster?"

When the plane arrived in Birmingham it was met by Fred Shuttlesworth. He drove King to the homes of the parents of the four dead children, where King did what he could to comfort them. The funeral was held the next day, in a church he had never visited before, but at the invitation of the minister, King was conducting the service. Having been introduced, he came to the pulpit to address the mourners.

For a moment he stood silently. Then he gestured toward the four child-size caskets. "We see before us a great triumph for segregation," he said heavy-heartedly.

From the people came sounds of weeping.

"The murder of four girls studying in Sunday school."

A woman sobbed.

"It was a terrible deed," he said. "But perhaps less terrible than the response of the community. I suppose it was too much to ask that it be officially said that the murder of children is wrong." He indicated the parents of the slain children. "I suppose it was too much to expect that one white official would attend the ceremonies so that their parents might feel better." He scanned the faces of the mourners. "As a matter of fact, except for white ministers from out of town, there isn't one white face here."

The weeping came in waves.

"Yet," King said, tears in his eyes, his voice breaking, "I still believe in nonviolence." He gestured toward the caskets again. "Consider this a down payment on freedom."

The mourners, sobbing, rocked from side to side.

"History has proved again and again," King told them, "that unmerited suffering is redemptive. The innocent blood of these little girls . . . may well serve as the redemptive force that will bring new light to this dark city. . . ."

At the White House, in the Oval Office, the President, the Attorney General, and the Attorney General's aide sat watching a television screen, observing Martin Luther King, Jr., as he conducted the service for the four slain black children. Their expressions were intense. The President was clearly angry.

When the service ended, the TV cameras began concentrating on the faces of the mourners. On a signal from the President, Beamer, the aide, rose and switched off the set.

"I want to go on television tomorrow night," John Kennedy said grimly.

Beamer's look showed that he disapproved. "I know what you're thinking," he said, "and I want to go on record against it. If you make a speech like that your chances of being re-elected are nil." He settled in his seat again. "I know you were moved by what King said—"

The President broke in. "Somebody has to use the moral power of this office to say that segregation is wrong." He smiled wryly. "Is that such a brave thing to do?"

"Yes," Beamer answered. "There have been other brave men in that chair. And they've been very clever and very careful how they reacted to this issue."

The President was silent for a second, looking thoughtful. "Maybe that's the trouble," he said finally. "Maybe we've all been too clever."

That evening John F. Kennedy gave the speech for which many people were to remember him most fondly; and it is perhaps the main reason that his picture stands in many black homes, along with pictures of his brother and of Martin Luther King. It was a simple speech, and Kennedy seemed ill at ease making it. But it was a landmark simply because no American President had ever put the moral force of the office behind the statement: "Segregation is wrong."

"It ought to be possible for American students of any color to attend public institutions without having to be backed up by troops," Kennedy told millions of Americans. "And it ought to be possible for American citizens of any color to register and to vote in a free election without fear of reprisal. But such is not the case. We say to the world and to each other that we are the land of the free. Does that mean it is a land of the free except for the Negroes? That we have no master race except with respect to Negroes? We are confronted primarily with a moral issue, as old as the Scriptures and as clear as the American Constitution. The heart of the question is whether *all* Americans are to be afforded equal rights and equal opportunities. Those who do nothing are inviting shame as well as violence. Those who act boldly are recognizing right as well as reality. Next week I will ask Congress to make the commitment it has not yet fully made in this century—the commitment to the proposition that race has no place in American life or law."

The President was not the only powerful man in Washington who had Martin Luther King, Jr., on his mind at that moment. In his office, J. Edgar Hoover, head of the FBI, was waiting for one of his agents to arrive with a report on the influence of the Communist Party on the black civil rights movement. He was anticipating being pleased with what the agent told him.

Hoover was seventy-seven years old now. The jowls of his bulldog face were beginning to sag, and his skin had a glassy tone. Blacks—in particular, Martin Luther King, Jr.—had become an obsession with him. His knowledge of blacks was limited to those in the Washington, D.C., area, who were allowed to be nothing but janitors and chauffeurs. He believed they should be restricted to that. To his mind, therefore, those blacks who rebelled were either dupes of the Communists or, worse, Communists themselves.

The agent, Sullivan, entered and approached the desk.

Hoover acknowledged his presence with a nod.

There was no small talk. Sullivan made no introductory comments. Standing, he read the report, page after page after page, his eyes fixed on the words. Had he glanced at Hoover, he would have noted that the more he read, the more sour the old man's expression became.

"There has been an obvious failure," Sullivan read, concluding the report, "of the Communist Party of the United States to appreciably infiltrate, influence or control large numbers of American Negroes in this community." Lowering the papers, he raised his eyes to Hoover.

The old man's expression froze him.

Sullivan swallowed hard, shaken.

"Dr. King?" Hoover growled.

"No reason to suspect him of being a Communist or Communist sympathizer," Sullivan replied, his voice suddenly small and pinched.

"This report," Hoover said acidly, "reminds me vividly of the reports I received when Castro took over Cuba."

Sullivan's face became ashen.

"You contended then that Castro and his cohorts were not Communists and were not influenced by Communists," Hoover reminded him. "Time proved you wrong."

"Mr. Hoover, I can only report my findings to you as honestly as I can. I spent a good many months working on this report."

"I know you have," Hoover responded, still glaring. "I know you've taken time away from other things that you could have been doing. That's why it's all the more a disappointment."

"I can't help it," Sullivan said, "if these are the conclusions I honestly reached." He made a feeble effort to redeem himself. "I pointed out that time alone will tell," he said. "I made it clear that the

Communists are trying hard to infiltrate the Negro movement."

Hoover snorted derisively. "Why are you trying to qualify it?" He gestured, dismissing the agent. "You've made your report."

Back in his own office, Sullivan discovered as he started to put the report down on his desk that his hands were shaking so severely that the sheets of paper were rattling. He realized that he was in deep trouble. Hoover's response to the report had been more than mere disappointment—it had been a threat. He knew that the Director was capable of dismissing a whole department. And Sullivan had responsibilities—a wife, children, a mortgage.

The agent could not sleep that night. Worry about his career kept him awake. And the next morning an incident occurred that compounded his concern for his future in the Bureau. He met Hoover in a corridor of the FBI building and, as was his custom, greeted the Director deferentially. Hoover did not reply. Worse, he did not even look at Sullivan. He passed Sullivan by as if he had already become a non-person.

Sullivan rushed back to his office. He summoned his secretary and dictated a memo to Hoover:

We regret greatly that the report did not measure up to what the Director had a right to expect from us from our analysis. But now we are stressing the urgent need for imaginative and aggressive tactics to be utilized through our counterintelligence program to attempt to neutralize or disrupt the Communist Party's activities in the Negro field.

We must mark Dr. King now, if we have not already done so, as the most dangerous Negro to the future of this nation from the standpoint of Communism, the Negro, and national security.

Two days passed, during which Sullivan fretted and agonized, before the Director reacted to the memo, summoning the agent to his office. Hoover had the memo in front of him on his desk when Sullivan entered.

"I can't understand how you can so agilely switch your thinking and evaluation," Hoover said cuttingly. "Now you want to load down the field with *more* coverage—in spite of your past evaluation. I don't intend to waste time and money until you can make up your mind what the situation really is."

Sullivan went back to his office and reported the conversation to Fraser, an agent he had known for some time and trusted.

"What does he want from us?" Fraser asked.

"What does he want from us?" Sullivan repeated, mockingly. "He wants us to tell him he was mild in his assessment of the influence of Communists on King and the Movement, even though there's no evidence that there is any. He wants us to out-Hoover Hoover. Get me the files on King's aides. If we can't find anything on King, maybe we can find something on them."

In years to come, the Church Committee would

ask Sullivan whether he thought what he was doing was illegal, unethical, or immoral.

"The matter of legality, morals, or ethics was
never raised by myself or anyone else," reported
Sullivan.

20

On one of his rare days of rest, King lay on the living room couch in his home, napping. Every once in a while he would suddenly waken, disturbed by a recollection of some terrible moment—the beating in the Montgomery jail, the stabbing by the woman in Harlem, the phone call about the bombing of the children in Birmingham—that crept into his subconscious mind. Gradually, however, the quiet of the afternoon calmed him, and his sleep became peaceful.

But even at home, serenity could not last long. Approaching the couch from behind, Yolanda and Marty had hands to their mouths, muffling giggles. Skullduggery was afoot. In the hand that she was not using to stifle her mirth, Yolanda was carrying a cup of water.

Reaching the couch, the children pulled themselves up and peeked over the back. Their father was lying on his side, a fuzzy purring sound coming from him. The giggles became noisy snickers. Carefully, Yolanda raised the cup and then tipped it, dribbling water into her father's ear. King leaped up, slapping wildly at the side of his head. The children exploded in laughter.

Their father spotted them. Digging water from

his ear, he spotted the cup in Yolanda's hand. Annoyed at having been wakened, doubly irked at having been made to look ridiculous, he saw red. "That was mean!" he shouted at the children. He grabbed at them—and missed. "Wait till I get hold of you!"

Delighted—not in the least afraid—Yolanda howled. "Run, Marty, run!" she called out, racing away.

And Marty ran, screeching as loud as his sister. But his was a cry of panic, not mirth.

The children disappeared, dashing through the living room doorway, headed in the direction of the rear of the house.

King's anger had lasted no more than a flicker of a second. He was laughing before the children had even cleared the room. Rising now, he roared in mock rage. "Where are they? When I get them," he boomed, setting out after them, "I'm really going to give it to them! Where's Yoki-poki? I know she wouldn't do it to her Daddy. It must be Marty!"

King went clomping down the basement steps. He heard Yolanda's giggling. But also—puzzling him a bit—he heard what sounded like whimpering. Then, arriving at the bottom of the steps, he saw movement behind the furnace.

Having trouble keeping his laughter in, King boomed out, "Where are they?" He moved on toward the furnace. "Marty! Marty!"

A small shadow sprang out from behind the furnace. King grabbed. He had caught his son. Marty struggled. Laughing, King tried to sweep Marty up into his arms. But the boy fought, screaming now. King realized all of a sudden that for Marty this was not play. The boy was terrified.

"What's the matter?" King asked, holding his son gently.

Marty, struggling harder, cried out for his sister.

Yolanda, as puzzled as her father, came out of hiding. At the same time, Coretta appeared at the top of the basement stairs.

"Marty, what's the matter?" King asked. "You're not really frightened of me, are you?"

His son broke free. Sobbing, he ran to his sister, dashed past his mother, then disappeared.

A bit later, Coretta went into her son's room. He was lying on his bed, hiding his face.

"Marty, why did you cry with your father today?" she asked gently.

His words were muffled. "They tease me because of him. They say, 'Your father's a jailbird.'"

"Do you know why he goes to jail?"

There was no reply.

"He goes to jail to help people," Coretta told her son. "Remember that day that you wanted to go to Funtown? Do you remember how you felt when we had to tell you that you couldn't go because you were black?"

He kept his face hidden, but she recognized nodding motions.

"Your father couldn't sleep that night. He had to go to Birmingham the next day, and he said, 'Tell him it isn't because he isn't as good as anybody else. Tell him he'll be able to go someday.'"

Marty raised his head, looking at her tearfully.

"So I think you ought to help him—because he doesn't like going to jail," she said. "He's as frightened by it as anybody else—and he's alone. He's very much alone."

Once more, the powers in the black civil rights movement gathered in the Oval Office. King was there, accompanied by Damon Lockwood. Also present were Roy Seeger and Paul Harrison. With the President were the Vice President and the Attorney General.

The meeting began cordially enough.

When the greetings were over, King addressed the President: "I haven't had a chance before . . . I want to thank you for what you said on television. It had never been said before."

"Thank you," the President replied perfunctorily. "But what I'm concerned about right now is this march you're planning. We want a civil rights bill, not a television spectacular. Supposing there's an incident?"

"There won't be any incident," Damon Lockwood reassured him.

The Vice President spoke. "I know these fellows on the hill," Johnson said. "I spent a good many years with them. You don't want them to say, 'Yes, I'm for the bill, but I'm damned if I'll vote for it at the point of a gun.'"

"If they don't want to vote for it," said Harrison, "they'll find a reason not to."

The President turned to King again. "What do you think, Dr. King?"

"I think it can serve a purpose. It can dramatize the issues for people who don't know about the issues first hand."

"It isn't the time!" Robert Kennedy said sharply.

King was amused. "Frankly, I have never engaged in any direct action movement that didn't seem ill-timed. Some people," he said pointedly, "thought Birmingham was ill-timed."

"Including the Attorney General," the President commented, glancing wryly at his brother. He shrugged. "Well, if you want to held the march, there's nothing we can do to stop you."

There were nods of agreement.

The President rose. "Thank you for coming, gentlemen. Dr. King," he said, as the others got up, "would you stay for just a moment?"

"Certainly," King replied.

When the others, except for the Attorney General, had gone, the President said to King, "Let's go outside."

The President walked out into the Rose Garden. King followed him, wondering why they couldn't talk about whatever it was in the White House. "Robert wants to talk to you," the President said.

"Yes?"

"It's about an advisor of yours," Robert Kennedy said, looking uncomfortable.

"Which advisor?"

"Stanley Levison."

"Yes . . . what about him?"

"Hoover says he's a Communist."

King now understood that even the President of the United States and the Attorney General were not without the fear that their own offices might be bugged.

King looked pained. "I thought we'd gone beyond that in this country," he said.

"Well . . . McCarthy's dead, but the melody lingers on," the President said glumly.

King gave him a steady look. "It's not true. I don't believe it."

Kennedy did not avert his eyes. "I've seen the files," he said. "There's enough ammunition there."

"What *kind* of ammunition?"

"People have said things about him. There are statements that he's made."

"People have said things about you, too," King reminded him. "And there are statements that you've made. Would you want to be held accountable for all of them?"

"We're not talking about me, we're talking about Stanley Levison," said Kennedy with a slight edge. "And I'm telling you that his statements can be used against him. And they can be used effectively." He looked hard at King. "You'll have to dismiss him."

King flinched at the notion. "That isn't so easy to do. He's one of the most valuable men in the Movement. In addition to that, he's a friend of mine."

"Dr. King," observed the President, "the southern strategy is going to be to say that the Civil Rights Movement is riddled with Communists. I have a civil rights bill I want to pass." He looked at King challengingly. "We can't take a chance on anything hurting that bill . . . can we?"

When he arrived back in Atlanta, King told Andy Young about his conversation with the President and the Attorney General with regard to Stanley Levison. The following day he held a private meeting with Levison in his office at the SCLC headquarters. Without preamble he told the attorney what he had learned from Robert Kennedy, concluding with the President's worry that Levison was a threat to the passage of the civil rights bill.

"There's no choice. I have to go." Stanley said.

"That seems to be what everybody thinks," King replied sadly. "These have been hard years for you, Stanley. You've had to work in the shadows—because there are racists among our own people who don't like the idea of a white man contributing so much."

Levison shrugged, dismissing that problem as unimportant.

"I owe you so much, I'll never be able to repay you," King said, looking away. "I remember when they tried to frame me on taxes. You said, 'It isn't up to you to defend yourself. It's up to us to defend you. It will be you against the State of Alabama, and the people will believe you.'"

"Those things don't matter," his friend said quietly. "Nothing must be allowed to hurt the Movement."

King shook his head. "I wonder if it's worth it. I wonder if, despite it all, I shouldn't call Hoover on this and face it out."

"You tried that once. It didn't work. He gets a better press than you." Levison rose. "The best thing I can do is get out of here." He hesitated. "Martin . . ." King saw, with pain, that he was struggling with himself to keep back the tears. "It's been the most inspiring experience of my life." Then, moving quickly, giving King no chance to change his mind, he went out the door.

King was still staring dispiritedly at the space that Levison had occupied when Andy Young entered the office a few moments later.

"What happened?" Young asked.

"He's leaving the Movement."

"I've talked to the Attorney General's people," Young said grimly. "Hoover has no evidence. He's lying. It's a downright lie. Stanley's not a Communist, and he never has been."

"I know. But we need that bill," King sighed. "We can't take a chance on anything hurting it."

"We need that bill," Young agreed. "But I wonder if anything is worth doing this to Stanley."

King was silent for a second, pondering. Then, "I think Stanley thinks it's worth it," he said.

21

Washington is a city of spectacle. Every four years there are imposing presidential inaugurations. But in its entire history, Washington had never seen a spectacle of the size and grandeur that took place on August 28, 1963.

Two hundred and fifty thousand people journeyed that day to the Capitol. They came from every state in the Union. They came in every form of transportation. They were good-humored and relaxed, yet disciplined and thoughtful. They were an army without guns, but not without strength. It was an army into which no one had to be drafted. It was white and Negro, and of all ages.

It was late, and there had already been many speeches when Martin Luther King mounted the steps of the Memorial. There had been much bickering back and forth as to when he should speak and how much. It was finally decided that Martin Luther King should speak last. Many people in the Civil Rights Movement wondered whether he would be up to it.

He was up to it. It was the crowning moment of the Civil Rights Movement until that time.

Millions of people watched and heard him; and it was the words of Martin Luther King they came away with.

"I say to you today, my friends, though . . . even though we face difficulties today and tomorrow . . . I still have a dream. It is a dream that . . . one day this nation will rise up, live out the true meaning of its creed: 'We hold these truths to be self-evident . . . that all men are created equal . . . .'"

The crowd had become quiet. So quiet, in fact, that, in its way, the silence was louder than the earlier murmur of conversations.

"I have a dream . . ." King went on, ". . . that one day on the red hills of Georgia, sons of former slaves and sons of former slave-owners . . ."

The people were beginning to respond. There was a mass edging forward. They wanted to miss none of King's words.

". . . will be able to sit down together at the table of brotherhood."

There were isolated cheers.

"I have a dream," King told them, his voice rising, "that one day even the State of Mississippi . . . a state sweltering with the heat of injustice . . . sweltering with the heat of oppression . . . will be transformed into an oasis of freedom and justice."

The crowd roared its approval.

When he spoke again, King's voice had a strength that it had never had before. "I have a dream . . . that my four little children will one day live in a nation where they will not be judged by the color of their skin, but by the content of their character."

"Yes!" shouted the thousands.

"When we let freedom ring," King told them, "black men and white men . . . Jews and Gentiles . . . Protestants and Catholics . . . will be able to join hands and sing . . . in the words of the old

Negro spiritual ... 'Free at last! Free at last! Great God Almighty, we are free at last!' "

The ovation exploded like cannons. People leaped high in the air, waving their arms, hugging each other, crying tears of joy. His name was roared: "King! King!" They took up his cry: "Free at last! Free at last!" The celebration went on and on and on, the chant swelling, spreading out, sweeping across the Capitol. And the radio and television microphones picked it up, and its thunder reverberated in every far corner of the nation. "Free at last! Free at last!"

In Congress, however, the cry for freedom was muffled in the traditional red tape. The civil rights bill stayed in committee, being given due consideration.

To keep it from becoming smothered, to put the force of public opinion behind it, King traveled from city to city and from town to town, speaking on behalf of the proposed legislation. The drain on his physical strength was tremendous. When he reached the point where he was traveling on spirit alone, his associates finally insisted that he rest.

On the morning of November 22, 1963, he was at home, in the living room, playing handball with Yolanda. King caught the ball that she had thrown just before it hit the glass doors of a cabinet.

"Close!" he said, making a face.

Yolanda laughed.

From upstairs came Coretta's voice. "What are you two doing down there? Are you turning the living room into a handball court again?"

King called up the stairs. "We don't have anywhere else to play. It's all right. We won't break anything."

King served.

Yolanda slapped at the ball. It sliced off at an angle, hit a wall, then ricocheted and struck a vase. The vase toppled. There was a crash.

"Martin!" Coretta protested from above.

Frantically picking up the pieces of the shattered vase, he called reassuringly, "It's all right. Nothing broke!"

Yolanda, watching him scramble, doubled over with silent laughter.

Coretta's voice cut it short. "Martin!" There was something different about her tone.

"It's all right," he insisted. He was hiding the fragments of vase under the couch.

"Martin. . . . Will you come up here. . . ."

King became aware of the change in her voice. Rather than annoyed, she sounded urgent, upset. He went to the foot of the stairs. "Is something the matter?"

"Come up . . . please. . . ."

"Back in a minute," King said to Yolanda, as he set out up the steps.

He found Coretta in the bedroom. The look in her eyes—shock—stopped him just inside the doorway.

"Kennedy's been shot," she said.

That evening King and Coretta, like most Americans, watched the endless TV reruns of Kennedy coming into Dallas. Kennedy making his final poignant speeches about Jacqueline. Kennedy riding in the motorcade.

King was terribly moved, more moved than he had ever thought he could be about the handsome Bostonian. It seemed to him that Kennedy's death was the quintessence of the tragedy of life. Whatever Kennedy had or had not possessed, he had something very few presidents ever had: vulnerability and the ability to listen. And King felt that he had died just as he was beginning to understand what life was all about, just when he was beginning to understand what the presidency demanded of him.

"This is the way I'm going to go," he said to Coretta.

"Martin!" She was frightened. "What are you talking about?"

"The sickness in this country," he said quietly. "It's deeper than we ever knew. I'll never reach my fortieth birthday."

Another call from the White House took King away from home. It came from the new President, Lyndon Johnson. It was a request for a private meeting.

When King entered the Oval Office, Johnson, an exuberant man, jumped up to greet him. "I'm delighted to see you," he said, directing King to a chair. "I've had every public leader worth anything in this room in the last ten days—Meany, Rockefeller, Henry Ford. But this is the moment I've been waiting for."

King peered at him in surprise. He had not been aware that he stood so high in Lyndon Johnson's esteem.

"There's been a great deal of rhetoric about civil

189

rights spoken here the last few years." Johnson could scarcely contain his contempt for the Kennedys.

"There's been a little more than rhetoric," said King, thinking of the dead President.

"Of course." Johnson made an offhand gesture. "But it's a long way from rhetoric to action. You and I are going to do some great things together, Dr. King." He beamed. "And I'm going to get particular satisfaction out of it because it's going to be accomplished by a southerner."

Johnson leaned back in his chair and smiled. King looked at him, wondering how to assess this crude, immaculately dressed, generous, and yet small-minded man.

A few days later, King resumed his schedule. Traveling constantly, he spoke wherever there was anyone to listen, pleading for support of the civil rights bill at one stop, demanding action—letters, phone calls, lobbying—at the next. As the weeks wore on, his body began to show the effects of the punishing regimen again. His associates' concern for his health increased with every speaking engagement. But he drove himself on. At last, on the verge of collapse, he went home again—this time to a hospital.

It was while he was recovering that his most notable honor was bestowed upon him.

One day Coretta received a call at home from an Associated Press reporter.

Talking fast, the A.P. man said, "We've just received word from Norway that your husband has been given the Nobel Prize for Peace for 1964. Is it possible for us to talk to Dr. King?"

For a desperate interval Coretta could not answer. Then she managed, "He's . . . in the hospital. . . ."

"I hope nothing's wrong," the reporter said.

"Just fatigue, that's all."

"You must be very proud of him."

Coretta said softly, "I am."

"May I call back for a comment?"

"Yes, of course," she said.

She hung up. For a moment she stood pensively, awed by the immensity of it. Then, her excitement growing, she dialed the number of the phone in her husband's room at the hospital. After several rings, the receiver was picked up.

"Martin?" she said eagerly.

"Mmmmmmm . . ." His voice was drowsy.

"How's the Nobel Peace Prize winner for 1964 feeling this morning?" Coretta asked.

"Fine . . ." he said absent-mindedly.

"Martin, did you hear what I said? You've won the Nobel Peace Prize!"

She heard the sound of gentle snoring.

Coretta laughed aloud. Then, carefully, so as not to disturb her husband's sleep with too loud a click, she laid the phone in its cradle.

At that moment, Yolanda and Marty, who had been playing outside, came into the house.

"Come here and sit down," Coretta called to them. "I've got something wonderful to tell you. This is—"

The phone rang again. When she picked up the receiver, her husband was on the line.

"Did you call me before?" he asked.

Amused, she prolonged the suspense. "Yes . . ."

"And did you say—"

But she could not contain her excitement. "Yes, Martin! The Nobel Prize!"

There was silence for a moment, and then King said slowly, "I wasn't sure. I thought I was dreaming. Are you sure it isn't a hoax?"

"No, Martin, it isn't a hoax. And do you know what it says? It says that they're wrong and you're right." Her voice rang with pride. "That's what it says, Martin."

In the months following Jack Kennedy's death, Robert Kennedy's conflict with two m-- escalated. The first was a man that he had respected from his youth, almost idolized: J. Edgar Hoover. The second was a man he had always despised: Lyndon Johnson.

Robert Kennedy had once, of course, been an aide to Joseph McCarthy and had for many years defended him as a great American. Kennedy's political odyssey was perhaps as great as that of any man in American politics. He had been goaded by King and the other black leaders to see Hoover as he really was. His vision was at its clearest after the time he called Hoover to ask how many blacks the FBI employed. Hoover wrote back: "We do not catalog people by race, creed or color."

It was assumed by Mr. Hoover that this would take care of Mr. Kennedy.

Robert came back with another very nice letter: "That's a laudatory attitude. You are commended to have it. But I still want to know how many Negro special agents you have."

Hoover consulted with William Sullivan. It so happened that during the war the FBI had five Negro chauffeurs, so Hoover had them made special agents. Now he did not give Robert Kennedy the courtesy of answering personally; he left that to Sullivan. Sullivan wrote Kennedy saying that the FBI had five Negro agents. Kennedy said it was atrocious: the FBI had 5,500 special agents, and only five were black.

Now, sitting on Robert Kennedy's desk, was a so-called "monograph." It was a compendium of wire tap reports, innuendo, and third-hand rumors about King's sexual life. Robert had gone through it amazed. What disturbed him most was the list of the people who had received it. They had received it without the consent of Robert Kennedy.

Robert picked up the phone and told his secretary to set up an appointment with Hoover immediately. Word came back that Hoover could not see him until the next afternoon. Fifteen minutes later, an incensed Kennedy stormed into the office of the FBI Director. Hoover's secretary tried to stop him at the door, but Robert strode past her.

Hoover, sitting at his desk at the end of the large room, looked at Robert silently. Nobody had ever entered that room without permission before.

Kennedy slammed the monograph down on the Director's desk. "Why didn't you check with me before you sent this out?" he demanded.

"I didn't see the necessity of checking with you."

"Will you tell me why it was necessary to send this to generals in the Army, to Adlai Stevenson, to Vice President Humphrey, to Rockefeller and to Johnson and Bill Moyers?"

"It was my judgment," Hoover replied, "that they needed to have it."

"Needed to have this character assassination? This compendium of scurrilous gossip and hearsay? Why?"

"It's good for them to know who they're dealing with when the crisis comes."

"What crisis?"

There was silence for a moment.

"The black insurrection," said Hoover quietly.

"Mr. Hoover, I know you've done a great deal of service to this country. But I think that for any man to have as much power as you have—and to have it for so long—is not only wrong, it's dangerous. It's *terribly* dangerous."

Robert Kennedy paused. He knew of Hoover's incredible power. He knew that to take him on as an enemy was tantamount to committing political suicide.

Robert walked around the room, telling himself: You must control yourself. You must control yourself. But he could not pull back now.

Hoover looked at him steadily, as though he were the one that had been treated unjustly.

"I want back every copy of this so-called monograph," Kennedy said.

"It's already gone out."

"I am ordering you to get them back."

Hoover stared at Robert incredulously.

"I believe I'm your superior," observed Kennedy.

Again, silence for a moment.

"No Attorney General has ever said that to me before," the Director said quietly. "No President has ever said that to me." He went on, his tone bitter. "I appreciate the high moral plane of your tenure, Mr. Kennedy. Except that you authorized wiretaps on your friend Dr. King yourself. I have it in your own handwriting."

Robert smiled his bright, tortured smile. "Yes, I did," he said. "I was wrong to have authorized them. I was thinking that my brother was mixed up with Dr. King in the public mind . . . and I was afraid that if Dr. King were discredited, my brother would be discredited. But my brother is no longer alive. I have nothing to protect now." He turned and started toward the door. "Besides getting back every one of those monographs," he said, "I want a letter from each of the persons who got it saying that they never read it." He glanced back. "I want it in writing. Is that clear?"

Robert strode out of the room and slammed the door. Hoover sat staring at the door.

22

In Oslo, Norway, receiving the Nobel Peace Prize, King said, "Modern man has built gigantic bridges to span the seas, and gargantuan buildings to kiss the skies. Yet in spite of these spectacular strides in science and technology, and still unlimited ones to come, there is a poverty of the spirit which stands in glaring contrast to our scientific and technological abundance. We have learned to fly the air like birds and swim the seas like fish, but we have not learned the simple art of living together as brothers."

At a small bridge on a road leading into Selma, Alabama, a march of blacks had come to a halt. Facing the marchers from the opposite side of the bridge was a squad of state troopers, some on foot, some on horseback. The tension was fierce. The blacks, demonstrating for voting rights, were determined to proceed. On the other hand, the officer in charge of the troopers, a dour-faced major, had firmly resolved that the marchers would not move one more step forward.

Addressing them through a bullhorn, the major ordered, "Turn about! Turn about and go back!"

Larry McKeecham, representing the SCLC on

the march, stepped away from the other marchers to confer with another SCLC observer. But before they had exchanged a half-dozen words, they were interrupted by the voice of the major coming over the bullhorn again.

"This is an unlawful assembly," he intoned. "You have ten seconds to disperse."

McKeecham stepped forward onto the bridge. "May we have a word with the major?"

The officer glared at him malevolently.

"We are protesting because we have not been allowed to use our Constitutional right to vote in Selma," McKeecham explained. "We are going to march to the capital to protest it."

"You have ten seconds," boomed the major. "One, two—"

As the counting continued, McKeecham rejoined the other SCLC representative. The other marchers crowded in around them, eager to learn what their decision would be. But in fact they had no options. Even if the consensus was to avoid confrontation, ten seconds was not enough time to begin a retreat. The decision had been made for them by the major when he started to count.

"Troopers forward!" he bellowed through the bullhorn.

The first line stormed across the bridge, clubs flailing. Terrified, the marchers huddled together. The clubs cracked against their skulls. Blood ran down their faces. The troopers hammered viciously at their bodies. The marchers shrieked in terror, trying to flee, dragging themselves away on broken limbs.

After the first onslaught, the troopers on horseback came surging across the bridge with a rebel yell. They rode straight into the huddle of marchers, scattering them, cracking limbs under the horses' hooves. The blacks who managed to break away were chased down by the cavalry and beaten to the ground. When the attack finally ended, the ground around the bridge was strewn with the twisted, broken bodies of blacks, soaked in their blood. The bullhorn had been silenced, the rebel yells expended; of the sounds of battle, only the moans and sobs of the victims remained.

In a private dining room of a hotel in Oslo, there was a party that included the King family, Andrew Young, Bernard Lee, Damon Lockwood, Mrs. and Mrs. Abernathy, and many other friends and workers who had been with the Kings from the beginning.

"I want to make a toast to God," King's father suddenly announced, holding his glass high.

They all laughed.

"A toast to God?" King said. "That's a little pretentious, isn't it, Dad?"

But King senior declared somberly, "My father was a sharecropper, and I wasn't able to finish college until I was a grown man with my wife and three children. I prayed to God to let them do the things I could not do. And God heard me. And in some kind of way—I don't even know how—He came down through Georgia and He laid His hand on me and my wife, and He gave us Martin Luther King." He raised his glass again. "And now the King family will go down not only in American history but in world history as well . . . because Martin Luther King is a Nobel Prize winner."

They all applauded.

Then King's mother rose.

The room became silent. Only on rare occasions did his mother decide to speak.

"I want to tell you a story about myself that I'm ashamed of," she said softly. "It's about the first time Martin spoke publicly. It was for a high school debate Martin had worked very hard for it. Martin talked so well that everybody there knew he had won. But he was black, and the other boy was white. So, of course, the white boy won." Her eyes became moist. "I'll never forget Martin's disappointment when he came home. And I said to him 'Martin, you're not going to change the world. You're just a little Negro boy.'" She sighed wistfully. "I was trying to keep him from what I thought could be heartbreak. I was afraid for him. I almost did what millions of other black mothers do all the time—make our sons less." Smiling, she looked at her son with pride as well as tears in her eyes. "But one man *can* make a difference," she said. "And that's why we're here today."

When King got back to the States, the talk was all about what had happened at the bridge at Selma King's next stop after New York was the White House.

"We need a voting rights bill," King told the President.

"We just passed a civil rights bill," Johnson responded defensively. "You're going too fast."

"People have to have the Constitutional right to vote."

The President remained reluctant. "Congress isn't ready for it yet."

"Then we have to make them ready," King declared. He looked at Johnson squarely. "We're planning a march from Selma to Montgomery."

Johnson leaned back in his chair, thoughtful. "I can't tell you this officially," he said, "but march."

"We'll need you to send in federal troops."

Johnson shook his head. "Not yet."

"You know what happened on the bridge."

But the President remained adamant. "Not yet," he repeated. "If we call out the troops now, we make a martyr out of George Wallace."

"Those are fifty of the most dangerous miles in this country for a black man to march, Selma to Montgomery," King insisted.

The President nodded agreement, but his mind was made up. "If you want a voting rights bill," he said, leaning forward to emphasize his words, "you're going to need pressure. A *lot* of pressure. Something big. Something spectacular. Something . . . like Birmingham."

"Some people *died* in Birmingham," King said sharply.

Johnson sat back. His expression told King that he knew full well what had happened in Birmingham. He offered no further comment, allowing his look to speak for him.

In a motel room on the outskirts of Selma, King, Andy and the others were planning the march.

"We march in the morning," King said.

"Is Johnson sending troops?" asked Andy.

"Not yet."

"Not *yet*? When? Anything can happen in any one of those fifty miles."

King shrugged. "There's nothing we can do."

"Martin, there's something *you* can do," Young said, his manner becoming even more concerned. "Don't march."

Something more than ordinary worry sharpened his tone. King looked at him in surprise.

"Jimmy Lee Jackson's gone," Young said. "Medgar Evers . . . Kennedy . . . Tom Moore . . . all gone . . . Now we have a tip that the Klan has hired someone to kill you."

King looked away.

"But it isn't just the Klan. You think the Nobel Prize has helped? It's made it worse. You're the biggest target in the country."

Damon arrived at the motel with a report on what the authorities would allow. "Judge Johnson has given you the right to march, but only fifty of you, and two abreast," he said.

"Why?" asked McKeecham, outraged. "It's suicide."

King swallowed the affront. He had swallowed affronts before. "All right," he told the others. "We're going to march fifty at two abreast, and we're going to march from here to the Capitol steps to insure that everybody has the right to vote. Get Archbishop Iakovos. Get Walter Reuther. Get Bishop Millard. They won't be able to go with us on the highway, but they can walk with us to the highway. And anybody that wants can join us in Montgomery when we get there."

"If we get there," added McKeecham.

When the lights went on, King jumped out of his bed. Fear was always somewhere near him. He could control it most of the time, but it was always waiting around the corner, waiting to engulf him. He hated it.

He was relieved to see Coretta sitting by the bed —relieved at first, then stunned, as he realized where they were and what was about to happen.

"What are you doing here?" he asked.

"I'm going to march."

King looked at the valise beside her; he saw the determination on her face.

"You're not going to keep me in the house this time," she declared. "Not this time."

"What about the kids?"

"The kids are all right. I left them with Mother and Dad."

Coretta went to the dresser to unpack. King watched her warily. "I guess there's no way to stop you," he said at last. He sat up in the bed and lit a cigarette.

Coretta studied his reflection in the mirror. "You look so tired," she said.

"You know, I can't even smoke in front of anybody else." He laughed faintly at himself. "I'm not a saint. I wish I were."

Coretta turned, her concern mounting. "Martin, what's the matter?"

"This march. This is the most dangerous march we've made. I know somebody's going to die on these fifty-four miles. It seems to need human sacrifice for every gain we make."

Coretta sighed. "It's a dangerous march, Martin but an important one. It's one hundred and two years since the Emancipation Proclamation, and yet college graduates can't vote in Selma, Alabama. Didn't you say that one of these days we would have a say in who is president of the United States? Give us the ballot. Isn't that what you said? It will change the history of this country."

King looked at her. "I know," he said. "But Corrie, isn't there some other way?"

People who witnessed it think it was the most exciting march of all time.

An enormous crowd gathered in Selma, including Walter Reuther, Archbishop Iakovos, and many thousands of well-wishers for Martin Luther King and his company, who would march fifty of the most dangerous miles in the South to the cradle of the Confederacy to confront the state government with the demand that everyone have the right to vote.

Watching it all was Deputy Attorney General Ramsey Clark. To him it was a security nightmare; there could be an assassin behind every rock, an ambush around every corner.

He watched King and his wife walking behind a one-legged man at the head of the huge procession.

To Clark, King's demeanor was incredible. He was smiling as though he were walking to a Sunday school picnic. And out there on that road, thousands of people were just waiting to kill him.

The marchers were singing, "Ain't nobody gonna turn me 'round, turn me 'round. Ain't nobody gonna turn me 'round, walkin' towards freedom's land."

When the marchers reached the highway, only fifty proceeded. The rest watched the lonely band move down the perilous highway.

The weather was cold, the road was muddy. They slept in fields, in the mush.

From time to time, an entertainer showed up to help them along. Tony Bennett was one of them.

A few days after the march had started, Tony arrived in Selma, where Bernard Lee met him with a car. When they stopped for gasoline, Bennett couldn't help but notice the hatred on the faces of the townspeople in the gas station. They knew what he was here for; and they could kill him for it. Looking at them through the car window, Bennett wondered about people's obvious need to hate.

There was a concert in a field lit by the headlights of Army trucks. Tony Bennett was only one of a number of performers. Also there was Harry Belafonte, who had done so much for the Movement, who raised money whenever King needed it, who felt so close to King. Other entertainers were Shelley Winters, Peter, Paul and Mary, Billy Eckstein, and Sidney Poitier.

When his turn came, Bennett stood on the small makeshift platform and sang "Just In Time." It seemed weird to him, singing in the dark, not knowing what was out there, so he just concentrated on King as he sang.

After the entertainment, King got up and thanked

all the performers in his quiet, matter-of-fact way. He told them how much he appreciated it.

Since then, Bennett has sung before royalty, movie stars, and at the White House, but nothing has meant as much to him as singing that evening in that muddy field on the highway from Selma to Montgomery.

23

Another person who wanted to help was Viola Luizzo.

Mary Winters, an attractive black woman who worked for the Movement, came forward as Viola entered the Selma office of the peace march. It seemed to Mary that Mrs. Luizzo had just driven, in her own car, a number of passengers from Selma to Montgomery.

"Is there anyone else that needs a ride?" asked Viola.

Mary laughed. "You back already? You've already picked up so many people. Where you from?"

"Detroit," said Viola. "I'm just a housewife. The only way I can help is to drive. It isn't much, but it's something."

"There's a boy who has to be picked up in Montgomery," said Mary. "He wants to join the march."

"What's his name?" asked Viola.

Claude was a gangling six-footer, wearing spectacles that tended to slip down his nose. He sat beside Viola self-consciously. He had still not adjusted to being in the same car with a white woman.

Viola sensed his shyness. "Are you a student?" she asked.

"In a way. I want to be. I want to attend barber school in Mobile."

"Barber school?" Viola smiled.

"You look tired," said Claude. "You want me to take over?"

"No. I'll be all right."

Suddenly a car was close behind them. It tailgated for a moment, then bumped into them.

"They must be crazy," said Viola.

Claude tensed, but said nothing. They drove a moment longer, and the car behind them dropped back a bit.

Claude spoke to pick up his spirits. "You have a place to stay in Montgomery?"

"I was going to make one more trip back." Viola laughed. "Unless I'm killed in the meantime."

She saw in the mirror that the car was coming up fast again. It swung out as if to pass, then drew alongside. Viola kept her eyes on the road.

There was an explosion, the sound of glass shattering. Viola fell forward. Claude tried to grasp the steering wheel, tried to hold onto it, tried to hit the brakes. The car swerved off the road, ran into a ditch, and smashed up against the embankment.

Claude switched off the ignition and lights. "Mrs. Luizzo!" he cried. "Mrs. Luizzo!"

Viola was slumped over the steering wheel. It was obvious she was dead.

The other car had turned and was headed toward them again. Claude leaned over Viola, closed his eyes, and pretended to be dead. He heard the car stop, a door open and close, and the sounds of two pairs of footsteps coming toward him.

A gruff voice said, "I don't think you hit him."

Even though his eyes were closed, Claude could sense that a beam of light was searching inside the car. He could feel Viola's blood dripping onto his hand.

"Baby brother, I don't miss," said a second voice.

Claude lay pretending to be dead until he heard the other car drive away.

He jumped out of Viola's car and ran down the highway. A truck was coming toward him. Claude stood in front of it, and the truck almost ran over him before it stopped.

Claude came to the side of the truck, shouting to the driver. "A woman's been shot! My God! She's been shot! There are men with guns around here! They just killed her!"

At first it seemed that only hundreds were going to show up in Montgomery. Then there were thousands. Over a hundred thousand. Exhaustion showed in their faces, a weariness of mind as well as body. They had been battered with taunts and epithets along the way. They had learned of the death of Viola Luizzo and had feared for their own lives. But they had survived.

More than survived, they realized, as they made their way through the city streets on their way to the capitol building. Along the way, crowds continued to watch them, but there was very little jeering from the sidelines now. Most of the whites still glared venomously at the marchers—but in silence. It was grudging respect for what they had done. Step by slogging step they had gained ground on the impossible, and now they had caught up to it. They were victorious.

Reaching the Capitol building, King climbed the steps and turned and faced his followers. The marchers were flowing onto the Capitol grounds and spreading out before him like an invading tide. Although their bodies were heavy with weariness, their spirits were lightening. In their eyes he could see the same spark of determination and dedication that had been there when the march began. In spirit, he realized, they were stronger now than when they had first set out.

From the steps, King spoke to them:

"Eight thousand of us started on a mighty walk from Selma, Alabama," he said, his voice choked with emotion. "They told us we wouldn't get here. There were those who said that we would get here over their dead bodies by ourselves." He looked out toward the far reaches of the vast crowd that had gathered on the Capitol grounds. "Let all the world today know that we are here . . . that we are standing before the forces of power in the State of Alabama . . . saying we ain't gonna let nobody turn us around."

They cheered, shouting proudly and gleefully.

"Today, I want to tell the city of Selma—"

"Tell them, Doctor!" a marcher cried out.

"Today, I want to say to the State of Alabama—"

"Yes, sir!"

"Today, I want to say to the people of America and the nations of the world . . . we are not about to turn around!"

They cheered again, their voices weary and hoarse.

"We are on the move now!" King assured them, his own voice growing stronger. "Yes, we are on the move, and no wave of racism can stop us!"

"Yes, sir!"

His voice throbbed with deep feeling when he spoke again. "The burning of our churches will not deter us! The bombing of our homes will not dissuade us! The beating and killing of Jimmy Lee Jackson will not divide us!"

"No! We will not be divided!" a man shouted.

"The shooting of Viola Luizzo, the mother of three children, will not stop us!"

"We will not be stopped!" came the response.

"The release of their known murderers will not discourage us! We are on the move now! Like an idea whose time has come. Not even the marching of mighty armies can hold us! We are moving to the land of freedom!"

"Yes, sir!"

King's tone softened a bit. "I know you're asking today: how long will it take? Somebody's asking, how long will prejudice blind the vision of men? I come to say to you this afternoon, however difficult the moment, however frustrating the hour, it will not be long. Because truth crushed to earth will rise again! How long? Not long, because no lie can live forever! How long? Not long, because you shall reap what you sow!"

"Yes, sir, how long?" they chanted. "Not long, yes, sir!"

"How long?" King called out. "Not long!"

211

"How long?" the marchers responded, their voices rising in a roar.

"Truth forever on the scaffold, Wrong forever on the throne!" King went on, in the words of the old hymn. "Yet that scaffold sways the future, And behind the dim unknown Standeth God within the shadow, Keeping watch above His own! How long?"

"Yes, sir!"

"Not long! Because the arc of the moral universe is long, but it bends toward justice!"

"Justice!" a woman repeated.

"How long? Not long, because Mine eyes have seen the glory of the coming of the Lord!"

"Oh, yes, sir!"

King's voice rose to its heights: "He is trampling out the vintage where the grapes of wrath are stored! He's loosed the fateful lightning of His terrible swift sword! His truth is marching on! He has sounded forth the trumpet that shall never call retreat!"

The marchers were pressing forward, eager to be as near to him as possible.

"Yes, sir!" they cried out joyously.

"He is sifting out the hearts of men before His judgment seat!" His voice was soaring now. "Oh, be swift, my soul, to answer Him! be jubilant, my feet! Our God is marching on! Glory hallelujah!"

"Glory hallelujah!" they responded.

"Glory hallelujah, glory hallelujah, glory hallelujah!"

The marchers sang out in exultation, "Glory! Glory hallelujah!"

"His truth is marching on!" King proclaimed.

And the jubilation was such that no single voice could possibly be heard above the others.

On Monday evening, March 15, 1965, the President of the United States addressed the Congress, seeking a voting rights bill. There was a certain familiarity about his words as he spoke to the Senators and Representatives:

"I speak tonight for the dignity of man and the destiny of democracy," Lyndon Johnson told the lawmakers. "At times, history and fate meet at a single time in a single place to shape a turning point in man's unending search for freedom."

He scanned the faces of the listeners.

"So it was a century ago at Appomattox. So it was last week in Selma, Alabama. This time, on this issue, there must be no delay, no hesitation, and no compromise with our purpose. What happened in Selma is part of a far larger movement which reaches into every section and state of America. It is the effort of American Negroes to secure for themselves the full blessings of American life. Their cause must be our cause, too."

He raised his eyes, looking beyond the faces of his audience.

"Because it is not just Negroes . . . but really it is all of us who must overcome the crippling legacy of bigotry and injustice. And . . . we . . . shall . . . overcome!"

24

The sand on the broad beach that fronted the luxury hotels was so clean and glistening that there was a rumor to the effect that it was taken in each night and laundered. King and his wife, dressed for swimming, had been strolling along that white shore for nearly a quarter of an hour without speaking. Such was the pleasure they felt in being alone together that they wanted to savor the rare, exquisite moment in silence. So they simply walked, watching the clean sand squeeze up between their bare toes—Coretta looking out over the rolling furrows of ocean, Martin squinting ahead into the bright sunlight to where rising air currents made the hotels appear to be swaying in some slight, mysterious breeze. They were in a world apart, unconscious of the other people on the beach.

Then a beach ball bounced past them, and as they watched it roll toward the water, their attentions gradually returned to the reality of the here and now. They smiled at each other fondly.

"You know," King mused, "I'd like to get a house so close to the beach that I could just simply roll out of bed and down the beach and into the ocean."

Coretta laughed. "We could become beachcombers," she teased him. "Think you'd make a good beachcomber?"

"I think I'd make the most wonderful beachcomber in the world."

They were silent again for several moments as he peered ahead, apparently intent on some distant view.

"I'm thinking about taking one of the positions they've been offering me," he said finally.

"Could you?"

"I don't know why I couldn't take off a couple of years."

She looked at him skeptically. "Do you really believe you could leave the Movement for that long?"

"Sure," he replied. "There's Andy. He's coming along fine. And Ralph. You know what I've been thinking? I wasn't home when our last three babies were born. Unless I do something I'll miss their childhood. I'll miss it forever."

"We'll see," Coretta said, not convinced.

But enough of family business. "How about a swim?" King suggested.

"All right!" she agreed, delighted.

They ran to the water's edge. As his foot touched the surf, however, King jumped and beat an instant retreat, howling in mock pain.

"What's the matter?" Coretta laughed.

"It's cold!" he complained. "I thought it was supposed to be warm here."

"It's still early. Come on," she called, going in deeper. "I thought you were supposed to be an athlete."

King retreated further. "I am an athlete. I just don't like cold water."

"It's fine!" she insisted.

"I'll wait for you here," he yelled over the noise of the surf.

Moving farther back, he sat down on the sand to watch as she began swimming leisurely along the beach line. As he waited, he listened with half an ear to the conversations of the people around him. Their main interest seemed to be the quality of service—or lack of it—in the various hotels along the beach. He was bored.

Suddenly a large pair of middle-aged white legs was standing in front of him. From the sunburned knees at his eye level, King raised his glance to the man's face. The pink skin was baby-soft.

"Boy. Can you get me a towel?" the man asked. The accent was New York.

Taken by surprise, King simply continued to peer up at him.

"A towel," the man repeated.

"I don't work here," King told him.

But King was never able to take any of the positions that had been offered him.

There was Watts.

And there was Vietnam.

Even people who had been followers of King began to wonder whether nonviolence had gone as far as it could go. It was true that people could board buses and go to lunch counters. But what good was it to go to a lunch counter if you didn't have a dime for a cup of coffee?

King decided that Chicago was the next place to

go. Chicago was held up to the rest of the country as a progressive town, yet those who lived there knew the bitter truth. And the man who held Chicago in the palm of his hand was Mayor Richard Daley. Daley was a master strategist who knew how to disarm adversaries; he would out-promise them, out-maneuver them, charm them, and then cow them.

Daley was not satisfied with just meeting King; he made King's arrival in Chicago an occasion.

"We want to welcome you," said the Mayor to the newspaper men and television cameras. "Chicago is a big town, and it likes to welcome big people, and you're one of the biggest. We welcome Martin Luther King, Nobel Prize winner who fights for the betterment of America. All right-thinking people share his views."

King nodded warily. This was not exactly what he had in mind.

"We have a whole schedule planned for you. A march through the Loop to Lake Front Drive, a joint appearance with me on some local talk programs, and the "Today Show," Daley continued.

Andy Young, who had accompanied King to Chicago, said, "Dr. King didn't come here to make appearances. He wants to talk about jobs and housing and schooling."

Ferris, a black man who was a close aide of Daley's, said defensively, "The schools and housing in Chicago are the best for blacks of any city in the United States."

The apartment at 1600 South Hamlin was no different from many of the other apartments in

218

Chicago's black ghetto. It was not clean; the paint was peeling off the walls, and there was almost no furniture.

Bernard Lee, pretending to be a lost soul from the South, looked through the apartment with an innocent, bewildered air. "How much do you want for this?" he asked.

"Ninety dollars a month," said Shavin, the white manager.

"That's a lot, isn't it?"

"Make up your mind. You won't get anything else at any better rates."

"I'll take it," Bernard said.

The next week King, Coretta, Yolanda, Dexter and Marty came to the apartment. King said quietly, "This is ninety dollars a month."

"Mommy, it smells here," Yolanda complained.

"Yoki," said Coretta calmly, "we're going to have to live here for a while. Most of our people live just this way."

Shavin, the apartment manager, entered, followed by Bernard Lee. Shavin was aghast. "You didn't tell me that Martin Luther King was in the building!" he said.

"We're going to live here," King said.

"I'll get some paint and new furniture and fix it up a little," Shavin told him.

"No," said King. "I want it just as it is. Just as it is."

Andy entered with newsmen and photographers. "Get a picture of this," he said, pointing to the stained walls and the soiled furniture.

The photographers did as Andy instructed, and Shavin looked nervous. He had visions of what the

219

white owner would say about what was happening.

Now the photographers were taking pictures of King and his family.

"This is our home," said King smiling.

Malcolm X sat in his austere, clean Chicago apartment looking at Martin Luther King, who sat before him. They had met before, had tried to find rapprochement. They respected each other a great deal, and yet they were on a collision course. And they knew it.

"It's nice of you to visit me," said Malcolm X. "I don't usually get such distinguished visitors."

"I want you to stop asking our people to burn down their own neighborhoods," said King.

"That's the last thing I would do. They're finding their manhood out there."

"I've watched you for a long time. What do you have to offer besides hate?"

"Hate is something to have," said Malcolm X, smiling. "Don't you think it's about time our people had hate?"

"Where does it take them?"

"It takes them to reality. It lets them know who the enemy is."

"So we're not better than they are."

"Who claimed we're any better?" asked Malcolm X. He smiled. "You're a racist."

King smiled.

Malcolm X looked at him for a moment, and his admiration was obvious despite their conflict. There was gentleness in his voice now.

"You've shown great courage. You've done more to desegregate this country than any man that ever lived. But you see, it didn't *cost* this country to integrate lunch counters or public accommodations. It didn't *cost* the country anything to guarantee the right to vote. But to end the poverty for black people and give them a chance to catch up will mean billions of dollars. And somehow I don't see that being done by appealing to their consciences."

Every word that Malcolm X had said had haunted King for a long time. "We'll find a way. But it'll be nonviolent," he said apprehensively.

"You still believe in the white man, don't you?" asked Malcolm X after a moment.

"I have no choice but to believe in him," King said quietly.

"I have a choice. I don't expect him to love me. I don't want his love. I court his hatred. I want no part of his society, no part of his values."

King studied Malcolm X for a moment, then spoke impatiently. "The dreary truth about the white man is that he is as flawed as everybody else. Not only do I object to what you're doing on moral grounds. I object to what you're doing on tactical grounds. If it comes down to a show of arms, we're only ten percent of the population. It's suicide."

"Maybe," replied Malcolm X. "But it's better than living this way."

"There's something else. There's nonviolent resistance."

"Are you still talking about Gandhi?" Malcolm X smiled facetiously. "You're not Gandhi. You're a middle class Southern boy."

"What I am doesn't matter," said King. "Why

don't you use your charisma, your brilliance, to help us live and not die?"

Malcolm X spoke almost in a whisper. "Because they hurt us too much. Because there is no way of living with them. Because they will deceive and hurt us in the end."

King stared at him. Then he said something that he had suspected for years and now was apparent to him. "The final truth isn't that you hate the white man. It's that you hate being black. You can't see beyond your personal rejection."

"This country respects violence," said Malcolm X. "Sometimes I think it's the only thing it respects. Hold on to your position, and you will be discredited. I can help the demonstrations in Chicago succeed."

King considered this for a moment. The combination of Martin Luther King and Malcolm X would indeed be a formidable one. One that white people couldn't crack.

"Modify your stand on nonviolence. We will appear nationally together. It will be the best thing for our people," said Malcolm X.

King shook his head. "I can't," he said. He paused and looked quizzically at Malcolm X. "At least you and I have one thing in common," he said. "We're both dead men."

The two of them sat silently for a moment. He had spoken what both of them knew.

"I love you," said Malcolm X. "You may not believe it, but it's true. I love you. You're a glorious fool."

King was enough of a vulnerable human being to wonder if it was really so.

King doubled his efforts to penetrate the ghetto, to understand it, and to make advocates. Among the places he and Bernard Lee visited was a pool hall patronized by the Blackstone Rangers, said to be one of the toughest black gangs in the country. A game was in progress as they entered.

At the sight of the strangers, the game stopped. The boys looked at him speculatively.

"So you're the Blackstone Rangers," King said. He gave no sign of being particularly impressed. "I hear you're supposed to be tough."

One of the teenagers recognized him. "It's King!" he said incredulously.

"You're kidding," said another.

"You King?" one of the teenagers asked doubtfully, approaching him.

"Forget that," King replied. "Who can I play with? I want to play the best pool player here."

"That's me," said a boy holding a cue.

"No, it ain't," another challenged, stepping forward.

"I didn't come in here to listen to you argue," King said. "I'm here to play pool. I want the best player here."

The boys laughed.

"Fred, you take him," one of them urged.

The boy with the cue grinned.

"Set 'em up!" King ordered, getting out of his jacket.

The balls were racked.

"Ten bucks on Fred!" a voice called out.

"I got ten bucks on the King!" a fat boy said exuberantly.

King, in shirtsleeves now, bent over the table and

lined up his stick on the cue ball. He shot. The balls broke beautifully, spreading out in all directions on the table.

"I believe," a boy with glasses said proudly, "the doctor is a pool player!"

Nearly two hours passed before King and Bernard left the pool hall. When they departed, King was buoyant and optimistic again. The easy, carefree hours with the black teenagers—laughing with them, bantering over the pool table—had revived him.

Minor demonstrations were carried out during the next few weeks. They made no big news, solved no big problems, but they got the attention of the city's political leaders, who saw them as a harbinger of larger demonstrations, more intense pressure, and the possibility of large troubles for the city of Chicago.

The mayor sent word that he wanted to meet with King, so once more King went to City Hall. This time there were no cameras, no microphones, no reporters present. With King was Andy Young. Mayor Daley had summoned a number of his political associates to back him up, but it was obvious from the beginning that they were merely props. Daley did the talking for the city.

"We're making progress," the mayor reported confidently. "We put on seventy new housing inspectors, and they've come up with a list of one hundred twenty-five housing violations. We're going to prosecute the violators." He handed a list to King. "See for yourself."

King passed the list on to Andy Young.

After a glance at it, Andy shook his head. "These aren't the real offenders," he said. "They're just small landlords."

There was an awkward silence.

Then Daley objected, "Chicago has lasted a long time. It's a tough city. You're not going to change it overnight."

"We've found that unless it's changed overnight it will never be changed," King countered.

Daley tried another tack. "We agree with all of your aims, Dr. King," he said mellowly. "It's just a matter of the art of the possible. We represent our constituents, and our constituents are troubled by the demands you're making."

"What demands?" asked Andy Young, his patience wearing thin. "Minimum wages? School desegregation? The dispersal of blacks from concentrated areas—ghettos—and the same renting conditions as for everybody else?"

"As I say," Daley soothed, "I agree with you and Dr. King. But you know how it is. There's a feeling around town among white workers that blacks have been getting too much and they'll soon be taking their jobs."

"That," King observed pointedly, "is because there are cynical people in politics and the press who prey on the people's fears—fears that have no foundation."

Before Daley had a chance to respond, Andy Young added, "I don't think we have any choice but to get as many people into our demonstrations as we can. To fill the jails. To boycott businesses that discriminate against blacks."

"I wouldn't do that," Daley advised. "This isn't Birmingham or Selma. You haven't been in Chicago before. There's a certain tradition here." He paused to look at each of them in turn, corralling their attention. "It was the home of Al Capone for years, you know."

25

In the living room of his home in New York, Stanley Levison sat deep in a comfortable chair. He was reading an account of the demonstrations by Chicago blacks in the *Times*. From the dining room came sounds of the table being set. Then there was a knock at the door.

From the dining room Levison's wife called, "Who is that?" There was mild annoyance in her tone. "Dinner is ready."

"Probably nobody," Levison replied, rising, folding the paper, going to the door.

Opening it, he was stunned. "Martin!"

"Hello, Stanley."

Levison had become speechless.

"May I come in?" King asked.

Levison hastened to recover his composure. "Of course!" he exclaimed, stepping back.

As King entered, Bea Levison, a slender, attractive woman, appeared from the dining room. She stared at him, surprised.

"Hello, Bea," he said, smiling warmly.

"Hello, Martin. What are— Will you stay for dinner?"

He shook his head. "Thank you. I only have a few minutes. I'm going to an NAACP meeting."

"Then you'd better eat," Levison said. "You'll need your strength."

"I guess you want to talk to Stanley . . ." Bea excused herself. "Nice to see you again." She returned to the kitchen.

"Sit down," Levison offered, motioning to a chair. "You look good!"

"Well . . ." King sat, then said abruptly, "Stanley, I'm going to jump off a cliff."

Levison laughed. "What are you going to do now?" he asked, seating himself opposite his friend. "Maybe I can stop you."

"I'm going to come out against Vietnam," King said.

Levison looked pained. "That *is* jumping off the cliff," he agreed.

"I've got to join those who are speaking out against it."

Levison thought for a moment, pondering the dangers. "As long as you know what it means," he said finally.

King smiled, pleased, but the pause that ensued grew uncomfortable. "How have you been?" he asked finally.

"Fine. Just fine."

King looked at him squarely. "Forgive me, Stanley."

Levison lowered his eyes, embarrassed. "There's nothing to forgive," he said.

"I should have kept you on, no matter what."

"It was my suggestion that I go, remember." Levison raised his eyes again.

"I need you," King said.

"*Need* me? You have advisors."

"None that knows the North like you do. And none that has your sense of history."

"There's still the FBI," Levison reminded him.

"Stanley, I want you to be my friend again."

"I always was, Martin."

"And let somebody try to make something out of it," said King.

From New York, King went to Atlanta for a few days of rest. While he was there, he told Coretta and his parents about his intention to speak out on Vietnam. His father held his peace on the matter until the final evening of King's stay. Then, when he and King's mother were at the house for dinner, he let loose, denouncing the idea.

"Do you *know* what you're doing?" he exclaimed, irate.

"Let's just enjoy our dinner," pleaded Coretta.

"Yes," King senior said, "but he has to know what he's doing! A black man doesn't venture out and give advice on foreign policy."

"I never thought of myself as just a black man," King said to his father. "Maybe I should. But I can't."

"They can frame you, you know. They can destroy you."

"Dad . . . they've done so much already."

"Let him enjoy his dinner," King's mother scolded her husband.

"I'm frightened for him," King senior protested. "I'm frightened."

Fear was elsewhere, too. But it was not so much for King personally as for the Movement that he had come to embody. He learned about the fear when he returned to Chicago and was summoned to a meeting of black leaders, among them Roy Seeger, Damon Lockwood, and Whitney Young, of the Urban League. Only Stanley Levison, who was also present, was taking in stride King's intention to denounce the Vietnam war.

Like King's father, Lockwood raged at him, "You know what you're doing? You'll destroy the Movement!"

"Lyndon Johnson is the best friend the black man ever had!" Roy Seeger added. "All he has to do is hear that you're going to make a statement like this!"

"Everything we've worked for these last eight years!" Lockwood went on in dismay. "Everything people have died for! You're going to throw it out the window for a gesture that will do no good!"

"How can you say that?" asked King. "Every day we see black boys coming home mutilated mentally and physically. Every night on your television set you see the destruction of hundreds of thousands of children with napalm. But even if it wasn't for black boys and brown children . . . even if it was only white people . . . I would still speak out."

Whitney Young looked at him contemptuously. "You always were a small-time clergyman," he said. "Don't get delusions of grandeur."

The others were shocked.

"Whitney!" Lockwood said in reproof, as hurt by Young's words as if they had been addressed to him instead of to King.

Whitney ignored the others' reaction, speaking to

King again. "All this talk about underfed children and the corruption of the system. You eat all right," he said. "If anything, you look overfed to me."

King's whole face became taut with anger, the muscles tightening into hard knots. But he managed to keep the anger under control and did not answer.

Damon Lockwood turned to Levison. "Can't *you* make him understand what he's doing?"

"I've told him what he's doing," Levison answered calmly. "He knows the consequences. He knows what can happen more than anyone else."

The others looked at King again, pleading with him with their expressions.

But his decision was firm. "Albert Einstein said," he observed, " 'The world is too dangerous to live in, not because of people who do evil, but because of people who sit and let it happen.' "

In Washington, President Lyndon Johnson was quick to register his opinion of King's plan to speak out against the war. He called Paul Harrison, King's friend, to the Oval Office. Would Harrison act as an intermediary and persuade King to remain silent?

"You know how I feel?" Johnson said, looking pained. "I feel as though a friend of mine, a friend I have helped, is putting a knife in my back and twisting it."

That seemed like an exaggeration to Harrison. "Why do you feel that?" he asked.

"You think what I'm doing in Southeast Asia is brutal?" Johnson asked. "You ought to know what my generals are *advising* me to do!"

"I see," Harrison replied dryly. "You're being humane."

"Nobody has helped the black people the way I have," Johnson said peevishly. "Nobody put the things that have been talked about into action. And now, when I need your support the most, when we're trying to do what's right, you turn on me!"

"You mean to say that we goddamn niggers are ungrateful," Harrison responded. "That's what you're saying, isn't it?"

The President stared at Harrison for a moment in cold fury, then turned away. The meeting was over.

The monograph that the FBI had prepared— implying King was a threat to the security of the country—and that Robert Kennedy had forced Hoover to recall, was now released to friendly newsmen and a few select Congressmen, university professors and clergymen.

In the offices of the FBI a letter was forged in King's handwriting, saying that the Southern Christian Leadership Conference was being investigated by the Internal Revenue Service on the suspicion that its funds were being misappropriated. Copies of the fabricated letter were distributed anonymously to the press.

A tape was prepared by the FBI. Its purpose was to show that King was unfaithful to his wife. Along with an anonymous note, the tape was mailed to Coretta. The hope was that it would break up the marriage, and, thus, in the eyes of his followers, King would be discredited and diminished.

In the King home in Atlanta, Coretta was in the kitchen clearing the breakfast table when the tape arrived. It was brought to her by Barbara, the girl who was helping her with the children.

"It came in the mail just now," Barbara said, handing the package to her.

As Coretta reached out to take it, a note dropped from the package.

"Here's something . . ." Barbara said, picking it up."

"What is it?"

Barbara began to read. " 'King. You are a fraud.' " She stopped, looking embarrassed.

"Is the note unsigned?" Coretta asked.

Barbara nodded.

"This isn't the first time this has happened," Coretta reassured her. "Go on—read it."

Haltingly, Barbara continued the reading. " 'There is only one thing left to do. You know what it is. You are done. There is but one way out for you. You better take it before your filthy, fraudulent self is bared to the nation.' " She raised her eyes from the note. "That's all." Then she looked at the tape that Coretta was holding. "Are you going to play it?"

Coretta answered with a question. "Is Martin still here?"

"He went to the office."

"Will you call him, please. Ask him to come home."

Nodding, Barbara left the kitchen.

Alone, Coretta began to tremble slightly. She looked around the room. "Are you listening to me now?" she asked angrily, speaking to the walls. "I know you've planted microphones. I've found them before. Are you waiting to see what I'll do? Are you waiting to hear me cry?"

Stifling the tears that were brimming in her eyes, she ran from the kitchen.

King found her in the bedroom when he arrived home. She handed him the tape and the note. He read the note, then looked at the tape speculatively.

"Have you played it?"

She shook her head.

He handed the tape back to her. "Play it," he said.

Taking it, she went to a wastebasket and dropped the tape in. "I don't want to listen to it," she said.

"Do you want me to tell you the truth about the rumors?"

"No." She moved toward him. "You don't have to tell me anything. Just . . . put your arms around me."

King held her tightly and kissed her gently.

"All I know is," Coretta said, "you're the most wonderful man I've ever known in my life. And you've been a wonderful husband and father to the kids."

"Coretta . . ." he said sadly. "I've made you suffer so much. I've never been home. You've all had to live with such danger."

"Martin, do you think I would have traded my life for anything? I can't tell you what it's been like to live all this time with you. Even the hard times. Even the worst times. You've taught me what being alive is. It isn't being afraid to love someone."

"The worst of times may be yet to come," he warned.

"Don't think that," she said, as if speaking the evil might bring it to pass.

"I guess I'm just tired," he sighed, sorry that he had frightened her.

"Martin—we'll be all right, won't we?"

"Yes," he answered. But he looked away. He had never been able to face her squarely when he was lying.

26

It was February 21, 1965.

The Audubon Ballroom in New York was jammed with blacks, most of them young and fiery-eyed. From the platform at the front of the big room they were being addressed by a woman whose duty at the moment was to introduce the main speaker.

"Without further remarks," she told the blacks, "I present to you one who is willing to put himself on the line for you."

As Malcolm X entered the ballroom, accompanied by two bodyguards, all eyes focused on him. He strode purposefully up the middle aisle toward the platform.

"A man who would give his life for you!" the woman continued. "I want you to hear, listen to, understand . . . one who is a Trojan for the black man!"

To the cheers of the audience, Malcolm X stepped up onto the platform, taking the woman's place. The sound of cheering rose, then, at his urging, subsided.

"As you know," the black militant began, "I have been blessed to visit the holy city of Mecca."

There was a murmur of approval.

"Since then, I have been able to understand things more clearly than I have before. I have seen thousands of people—black, brown, and white—practicing the same ritual . . . working toward the same goal. Growth is change," he said, giving the words special emphasis. "And I no longer condemn the white man for being evil . . . although I do condemn them collectively for what they have done to our people."

There was stirring near the rear of the auditorium. Malcolm X glanced fleetingly in the direction of the sound, then fixed his attention on his audience once again.

"What I understand more clearly than before," he said, "is that this society—this American society —has produced and nourishes the psychology which brings out the lowest and most base part of human beings."

An argument suddenly broke out between two men seated near the center of the auditorium. They were on their feet, shouting, one accusing the other of picking his pocket, the other denying the charge. The eyes of the audience had, of course, shifted to the two men who were arguing.

Malcolm X called out to them, "Hold it! Don't get excited. Let's cool it, brothers."

Suddenly, three men in the first row sprang to their feet. Each man held a pistol, and each pistol was aimed straight at Malcolm X. With most of the audience watching the fight in the center of the auditorium, Malcolm X was one of the few present who saw the guns. Shocked, he stared at the pistols and the gunmen for only a split second.

Then the shots rang out, round after round.

On the platform, Malcolm X's body jerked violently, once, twice. Then his head exploded like a ripe melon.

Screaming, the assembly dissolved into panic. Another leader was finished. The chaos would go on.

In Atlanta, King senior entered the pastor's study of the Ebenezer Baptist Church. He moved slowly, quietly. His son was seated at the desk, writing, preparing a sermon. Preoccupied, King junior glanced up momentarily as his father entered, then returned his attention to his work. The older man sat down in the chair that faced the desk. He sat in silence, his expression sorrowful and thoughtful.

The silence, uncommon when King senior was in a room, soon began to act as an irritant on King junior. Distracted, he raised his eyes to his father, looking at him questioningly, knowing that he had something on his mind.

"Malcolm's dead," King senior said.

King put his pen down. "Dead?"

"He's been killed."

"How?"

"He was shot. He was making a speech." The old man gestured futilely. "Nobody seems to know where the shots came from . . . all over, they say. . . ."

King put a hand to his eyes, covering them. "Who did it?"

"Some black men in the place."

King lowered his hand, looking at his father with

disbelief. "Black men? *Black men* killed Malcolm?"

His father nodded. "They don't know who or for what reason yet."

King sat back, stunned. "Malcolm dead . . ." he murmured. "I can't believe it. We fought . . . but I was never in doubt about his stature. I can't believe a world without Malcolm." He suddenly hiccupped. He started to speak again, but another hiccup came out in place of the words. "I think—" he began, but could not go on. He was shaken by a long series of spasms.

King senior was shaken. "Son, what's the matter?"

King gripped the arms of the chair and held his breath.

"What can I do for you?"

Cautiously, tentatively, King released the breath. "I'll be all right, Dad," he said.

"I'll get somebody else to preach your sermon for you today," his father offered.

King hiccupped again. But he shook his head. "No, I'll do it."

They were both silent for a few moments, waiting for the spasms either to end or become more severe. When no more hiccups came, King senior spoke again, but on a different subject, suspecting that it was the news of Malcolm X's death that had brought on the seizure.

"I'm going to discharge that new deacon," he said gruffly. "I heard him making comments about you, repeating that filth."

"No, don't fire him," King replied. "I'll speak to him."

King senior rose. "All this time, and you still don't

know how to deal with your enemies," he growled. Halfway out the door, he turned and repeated his offer of assistance: "I could get somebody to give your sermon . . ."

"It's all right," King assured him.

When his father had gone, King picked up the pen and began writing again. But he kept at it for only another few minutes. Then he tossed the pen aside, picked up the sermon he had been writing, wadded it into a ball, and dropped it in the wastebasket.

A short while later when he entered the pulpit he spoke not from a prepared text but from his heart.

"Every now and then," he told the congregation, "I think about my death."

His words brought a low murmur of surprise from the parishioners.

"I don't think of it in a morbid sense," he qualified, smiling faintly. "I ask myself what I would want said. If any of you are around when I have to meet my day . . . I don't want a long funeral. And tell them not to mention that I have a Nobel Peace Prize. Tell them not to mention where I went to school. None of that is important.

"I'd like somebody to mention that day that . . . Martin Luther King, Jr., tried to give his life to serving others . . .

"I'd like for somebody to say that day that . . . Martin Luther King, Jr., tried to love somebody . . .

"I want you to say that day that . . . I tried to be right on the war question . . .

"I want you to be able to say that day that . . . I did try to feed the hungry . . .

"I want you to be able to say that day that . . . I did try in my life to clothe those who were naked . . .

"I want you to say on that day that . . . I did try in my life to visit those who were in prison . . .

"Yes, if you want to say that I was a drum major, say that I was a drum major for justice! Say that I was a drum major for peace! And all of the other shallow things will not matter.

"I won't have any money to leave behind. I won't have the fine and luxurious things of life to leave behind. But I just want to leave a committed life behind.

"That's all I want to say. If I can help somebody as I pass along . . . if I can cheer somebody with a word or song . . . if I can show somebody that he's traveling wrong . . . then my living will not be in vain.

"If I can do my duty as a Christian ought . . . if I can spread the message as the Master taught . . . then my living will not be in vain."

He stepped down from the pulpit. For a moment there was absolute silence, and then, softly, the choir began to sing.

King's sermon on the prospect of his death heightened Coretta's concern for her husband. She tried to force the thought of losing him out of her mind by keeping continually busy. On the afternoon of the sermon, while he was resting, she went to the SCLC office to see if there was something there that she could do to help. She found Stanley

Levison alone in the office, sorting through the week's collection of press clippings on the SCLC and King. Coretta offered to assist him with the chore.

"I'm not so sure that's a good idea," he replied. "They're not all complimentary, you know."

"I've been cursed and spit on because I'm his wife," she reminded Levison. "Words, as the saying goes, will never hurt me."

Laughing, he handed her a batch of the clippings.

Looking at the first one, Coretta winced. It was a cartoon of King, in which he was depicted as a fat ape. The caption read, "Now Ah'm gonna tell ya all what to do about Vietnam." She grimaced, then sat down at a table and began reading and categorizing the rest of the clippings.

"Ummm . . ." Levison said musingly.

"What?" Coretta asked.

"From the *New York Times*," Levison replied. " 'Dr. King is misguided in his appraisal of Vietnam.' I wonder if it ever occurred to the *New York Times* that the *New York Times* might be misguided?"

"I'm sure not."

A moment later, Levison gave a sudden growl of surprise and anger.

"What now?" she asked.

"Nothing," he answered quickly. He was hiding what looked like a magazine article under the pile of other clippings.

Coretta got up and went to him. "What is it?" she asked.

Reluctantly, he retrieved the article, which consisted of several magazine pages, and handed it to her.

"It's by Damon," she remarked, beginning to read as she walked back toward the table. "How could you be upset by anything—" She interrupted herself. "No . . . this can't be Damon's writing . . ." she said, incredulous, sitting down at the table to finish the article.

Levison watched her for a moment as she read. As the look of hurt in her face deepened, he had to turn away.

The next day, taking the article with her, Coretta went to Lockwood's office. His secretary asked her to wait, then stepped into Lockwood's private quarters. When the secretary returned, she looked apologetic.

"He's busy right now," she told Coretta.

Coretta moved on past her and opened the door to Lockwood's private office. He was alone, sitting at his desk.

"Are you sure you don't have a few minutes for me, Damon?" she asked with sarcasm.

"All right . . . come in . . ." he assented grudgingly.

She entered and closed the door, then dropped the magazine article in front of him on his desk.

"I didn't want to write that," he said, avoiding her eyes. "I had to."

"You *had* to say that Martin's friends will never again listen to him or be moved by him the way they were before?"

"Yes. I believe that." He faced her straight-on at last. "Coretta, I have a great affection for Martin . . . as much affection as for any man I've met in my life. But he's done the Movement a great harm. A harm it may never recover from."

"Why? How?"

"He's alienated Johnson," said Lockwood. "He's put a slur on black patriotism."

"You don't believe that."

"Yes, I do." His eyes shifted away from her again. "I believe this is a necessary war," he said. His manner had suddenly become mechanical.

"You don't believe that for a moment," she countered instantly. "Damon, you're one of the brightest men I ever knew. You know that this is the most unjust and brutal war in our history." She sat down on the edge of the chair that faced his desk. "Shall I tell you what it is, Damon? You're fifty. And you're frightened."

"We're all getting older," he said vaguely.

She considered, thinking, maybe it wasn't as simple as that. "What did they give you, Damon?" she asked softly. "A place in the administration? A grant? What?"

He did not answer.

"Black boys are being killed . . . and they're killing for no reason . . . and black leaders are not speaking out," Coretta said, exasperated. "One of these days, black leaders are going to look back and see that there was no greater crime ever committed on black people than Vietnam. By that time, no one will remember. But *you'll* remember, Damon."

He remained silent.

She rose. She started to retrieve the magazine article, then changed her mind. "I'll leave it for you . . . to think about," she said. Then she left the office.

At the sound of the office door closing, Lockwood turned his eyes to the magazine article. He picked it up and stared at it bleakly, knowing he would never be the same man again.

27

Summer, 1966.

In Chicago, the gains for blacks remained miniscule, superficial. Mayor Daley, promising change, retained the status quo. When blacks demonstrated, he gave them what he referred to as police protection; in fact, the "protection" was an armed ring around them, containing them in the ghetto and therefore neutralizing them. Daley's guile was doing what southern hate had never been able to do. The blacks, it seemed, were checkmated.

But there was one possibility for breaking his wily siege. The decision was made by the black leaders to march into a white area of the city where resistance to their aspirations was most fierce, where blacks were barred from housing, where it could be dangerous for a black to be seen on the streets. King came to Chicago to lead the march, bringing with him Andy Young and Ralph Abernathy. With hundreds of blacks behind them, and Neal Price, the local black leader, beside them, they set out on foot to invade the Marquette Park section, the area that most clearly symbolized Chicago's resistance to their needs and rights. Escorting them were Daley's police.

The whites were waiting for them, lining the

streets. Here, there was none of Daley's cleverness. It was the South all over again. There was raw hate on the faces of the whites. They cursed, they threatened. They pressed in on the marchers from the curbs and retreated only when the police drew their guns and ordered them back.

Suddenly, the commander of the police called the march to a halt. While the marchers marked time, jeered by the bystanders, the police commander sent a squad of officers on ahead. The officers surrounded a tree, pointing their guns upward toward the branches. A surly young man came climbing down. He was carrying a rifle. The police hustled him away.

The march resumed. The tension was electric. The police kept their guns drawn.

"Go back where you came from!" the whites shouted.

"We don't need black power! What we need is dago power!"

"Go home! Go home! Go home! Go home!"

A rock hit King in the face. Instinctively, he threw up his arms to protect himself.

The whites cheered the rock thrower.

Police surrounded King.

A reporter who was covering the march handed King a handkerchief. As he wiped the blood from his face, the reporter asked, "Are you all right?"

King smiled faintly. "I've been hit so many times I'm immune to it."

"You can't go on. It's too dangerous. I've never seen anything like this."

"Oh, no. We can't stop the march. We're going on," said King, who had seen danger before, but who was very much aware, nonetheless, of the heaviness of tonight's menace.

Again the trek through Marquette Park resumed. Rocks and chunks of brick were hurled at the marchers. Persistently the whites pressed forward to get at the marchers. When the police pushed them back in one spot, they surged forward in another. There were isolated clashes between blacks and whites, broken up by the police. Still the blacks advanced.

Ahead, there was a sudden flash of flames. A car had been set afire. A squad of police raced toward the fire. Another car burst into flames. As more police set out after the arsonists, the march became vulnerable. The whites attacked, the blacks fought back. Blood ran; heads were broken. The police regrouped and waded into the battlers, swinging their clubs indiscriminately, beating blacks and whites alike.

The march was a disaster.

Several days later, the black leaders gathered in King's Chicago apartment to receive a report from Neal Price, who had met with the mayor.

"Daley's willing to give us a commission on open housing," Price reported. "He doesn't want any more Marquette Parks, either."

There was no response from the others except looks of disappointment.

"It isn't what we started out for," Price said. "But no one else could have gotten it."

"I can't forget the faces of those people in Marquette Park." King shook his head. "People from Mississippi should come here to learn how to hate."

"Did you think it was only in the South?" Stanley Levison asked gently.

"I didn't know the extent of it here," King confessed. "What is it in American people that makes it necessary for them to hate? Why is it so necessary to look down on someone?" He sighed dismally. "If only they could understand that the more progress we make, the better it is for them . . . that we're fighting the same battle."

"Will you accept the conditions?" Neal Price asked him. "No more marches, open housing?"

King nodded. "Yes . . ."

"It's a beginning," Price said. "It's a victory in a way."

"It's a defeat," King disagreed. "We may tell others that it's a victory. But it's a defeat, and we know it." He looked at the others. Their expressions confirmed his own opinion. "Daley outmaneuvered us," he said. Then he smiled softly. "But we'll be back."

The defeat in Marquette Park had consequences for King personally that he had not anticipated. In New York, not long afterward, as he began to address a rally of young people, he sensed a certain antipathy emanating from the audience. And his reception, when he had been introduced, had been unusually subdued.

"We are at the moment," he said, beginning, "when our lives must be placed on the line if our nation is to survive its own folly. The war in Vietnam is just a symptom of a far deeper malady within the American spirit."

Pausing, he looked out at the young faces. They were expressionless.

"I am convinced," King went on, "that we as a nation must undergo a revolution of values. We must rapidly begin to change from a thing-oriented society to a person-oriented society. When machines and computers, profit motives and property rights are considered more important than people, then we are in deep trouble."

There was no response at all.

"True compassion is more than flinging a coin to a beggar. A true revolution of values will look uneasily on the glaring contrast of poverty and wealth. A true revolution of values will lay hands on the world order and say of war, 'This way of settling differences is not just. This business of burning human beings with napalm . . . filling our nation's homes with orphans and widows . . . injecting poisonous drugs of hate into the veins of peoples normally humane . . . sending them home from dark and bloody battlefields physically handicapped and psychologically deranged . . . cannot be reconciled with wisdom, justice, and love.'"

From somewhere in the crowd came a hoot, hardly audible, but King heard it. He stiffened slightly. When he spoke again, there was an undercurrent of hesitancy in his voice.

"A nation that continues year after year to spend more money on military expense than on programs of social uplift . . . is approaching spiritual death . . ."

The young people booed him.

Back in Chicago, at another rally, he was booed again when he expressed the same views. Since it could not be his *words* they were scorning, it was *him*, he realized, and the nonviolence that he stood for. To this audience, he and it were failures.

He shouted back at them. "Oh, no!" His voice was like thunder. "I'm not gonna allow anybody to pull me so low as to use their methods to perpetuate evil throughout the system!

"I'm sick and tired of violence!

"I'm tired of the war in Vietnam!

"I'm tired of war and conflict in the world!

"I'm tired of shooting!

"I'm tired of hate!

"I'm tired of selfishness!

"I'm tired of evil!

"I'm not gonna use violence, no matter who says so!"

28

Congress had cut back on portions of the anti-poverty program, particularly food stamps. King had heard about the terrible effect the retrenchment was having on the blacks in the economically depressed back-country areas of the South. He went to see for himself, accompanied by Andy Young and other leaders of the SCLC.

In Marks, Mississippi, one of the poorest communities in the United States, they found starvation and hopelessness. Children with distended stomachs plodded through the red dust, moving like old men. And the old men did not move at all; they sat, remembering the most wonderful times of their lives—when they had work to do. Poverty was a plague that had settled on the area, dulling minds and wasting bodies.

"If only Congress would come down here and see what's happening," one of the SCLC leaders lamented.

"Congress will never come down here," King replied. "But maybe we can take these people to Congress."

"What are you talking about?"

"I'm talking about taking these people to Washington," King said, angered by the suffering he was seeing. "A march on Washington. A poor people's march."

The leaders returned to Atlanta. Plans for the march were made, then a press conference was held at SCLC headquarters. King faced the reporters.

"The Poor People's Campaign," he told them, "will be drawn from Roxbury in Boston to Lawndale in Chicago to Marx in Mississippi to Wheeling in West Virginia to Hollister in California. The campaign will consist not only of blacks, but Puerto Ricans, Mexicans, Indians, poor whites, Appalachians."

"Dr. King," asked a woman reporter, "what do you intend to accomplish by this?"

"We will place the problem of the poor," King explained, "at the seat of the government of the wealthiest nation in the history of mankind. If that government fails to acknowledge its debt to the poor, it will have failed to live up to its promise to the life, liberty, and pursuit of happiness of its citizens."

"Don't you think you'll get a great deal of criticism?" a bald-headed man asked. "There's a lot of backlash about the danger of the welfare state."

"These people want jobs, not handouts," King answered.

"What are you going to do if there are incidents of violence in the capital?"

"There will be no incidents of violence."

"The whole concept of nonviolence is being questioned even among your own people," a young reporter remarked.

"If I will be the last person in this country to speak for nonviolence," King told him, "I will be that person."

In Memphis, in a pouring rain, a city sanitation truck pulled into the yard and stopped. The two black men who were riding on the back of the truck jumped down. They had been working the truck in the downpour for hours, feeding garbage into its crusher, and they were drenched. There was a grinding of gears. Waiting, as the steel teeth of the crusher came down, they removed their jackets and draped them over their heads in a futile attempt to shelter themselves from the hard-driving rain.

When the crusher had done its work, the driver of the truck, a white man, jumped down from the cab and ran to the office. The two black men, Jake Snipes and Harry Sylvester, continued to stand in the rain for a few moments. Then, hesitantly, they walked toward the office, where the white sanitation workers were waiting out the downpour. As the blacks approached, the whites' conversation came to a standstill. Snipes and Sylvester paused in the open doorway.

The white foreman called out to them, his voice surly. "What are you two doing in here?"

"It's raining like hell out there," Snipes answered.

"You know the rules," the foreman said. "You're not allowed to hang around in here."

As Snipes and Sylvester turned away, leaving, the conversations of the white men resumed.

Outside again, they ran through the rain to the truck they had been working. When they tried to get into the cab, they found the doors locked. They ran on to the next truck. Its doors were locked, too. Finally, after a fruitless search for a cab with an unlocked door, they crawled into the back of a truck that had its crusher open. There, deep in the maw of the crusher, they at last escaped from the rain.

As the two black men sat talking dispiritedly, soaked, staring out at the driving downpour, there was suddenly a spark. It could have been the reflection of a flash of lightning. Then came a rumble of gears that could have been mistaken for thunder. Abruptly, the two men realized that the jaws of the crusher were closing on them. For a second they were immobilized by shock. Then it was too late to escape. The teeth of the crusher were bars, imprisoning them. They screamed madly. Then the only sounds were the grinding of the crusher's teeth and the battering of the rain.

A few days later, Reverend Williamson, a black leader in Memphis, arrived in Atlanta to discuss with King the deaths of Snipes and Sylvester.

"They just wanted to get in out of the rain," he said, as they sat together in King's office at SCLC headquarters. "But that was against the rules. Black garbage workers in Memphis can't wait in the office when it rains."

"What about their families?" King asked.

"They aren't entitled to any kind of compensation. Their families get nothing."

Andy Young entered the office.

"Jerry's talking about those two men who were killed in Memphis," King said, looking up at Young.

"We tried to march on Monday," Reverend Williamson said. "We went down Main Street to have a demonstration at the Mason Temple. They maced us."

"They want me to come," King explained to Young.

"Can't do it," Young said. "We're scheduled to arrive in Washington on the Poor People's Campaign on the twentieth."

"All we're asking him to do is take a walk downtown, make a speech, go back to the airport," Reverend Williamson begged. "It shouldn't take more than an hour and a half."

"Martin, we shouldn't take any detours," Young objected. "We have enough on our hands."

"It would be the biggest thing in their lives," Reverend Williamson said hopefully to King.

"When were you planning it?" Young asked him.

"Wednesday."

"We don't have time to prepare security," Young argued.

"There's no problem with security," Reverend Williamson assured him.

"Doc—" Young began again. Then he realized that he was wasting his breath. King had already decided to go to Memphis.

Marching with the sanitation workers in Memphis, on that March day in 1968, King was startled to hear cries of derision shouted at him by some of the young blacks who stood watching from the sidewalk. Suddenly, shoved from behind, he fell to his hands and knees. As he was being helped to his feet there was the sound of shattering glass. The

257

marchers began to panic. Reverend Williamson came hurrying up, arriving from the front line of the march. Around them the march was breaking up. There was an explosion of gunfire.

"We're getting out of here!" Bernard Lee told Williamson, urging King forward.

King resisted. "Maybe it will be all right," he said.

But Lee was adamant. "It's not going to be all right. I'm taking you out of here!"

Lee and Andy Young hustled King away, with Ralph Abernathy and Larry McKeecham clearing a path for them. The crowd shoved and cursed. The acrid odor of tear gas hung in the air.

When a car appeared, Lee shouted to the driver, "We have Dr. King here! Can we use your car?"

The driver, a black man, began opening the doors.

As King and the others were getting in, a young black man came rushing up. "I'm Detective Redditt," he told them. "Follow me. I'll get you through."

With Redditt leading the way on foot, the car began a slow crawl through the crowd.

"What happened?" the driver of the car asked.

"We don't know," Lee answered. "We heard shots."

King leaned across Ralph Abernathy, looking out a window. He saw a young black man lying dead on the sidewalk. As he peered sorrowfully at the lifeless figure, there was self-recrimination in his expression, as if he were blaming himself for the death and rebuking himself for deserting his fallen compatriot.

King was exhausted when he and the others returned to Atlanta. He slept for hours, and Coretta worried about him. But that evening when she went to his room, he was awake again, sitting up, staring out a window. Talking with her about what had happened in Memphis, he charged himself with the responsibility for the young black man's death. Nothing she said could relieve him of his sense of guilt.

While they were talking, Coretta heard voices coming from downstairs, a group of SCLC leaders arriving for a meeting. She left her husband to tell them that he was still too exhausted to join them. Shortly, however, while the men were still present, King appeared on the stairs, doing his best to look rested.

"What is this, a wake?" he asked, reacting to the looks of worry on the faces of the others. "I'm starving," he said to Coretta, descending the steps. "What about getting us something to eat?"

The group moved into the dining room. As the food was brought in, King seemed to revive. His mood became reflective. The talk turned to the past twelve years.

"The scariest time, I think," Ralph Abernathy said to Andy Young, "was in Philadelphia, Mississippi, and you asked me to say that prayer."

"You said it with your eyes open," Andy Young reminded him, laughing.

"I'm afraid I did, Brother Young."

"And then you said, 'Who knows? The murderers of Goodman, Chaney and Schwerner might be somewhere near.'"

"And they said, 'They're right behind you.'"

"Chicago was the worst for me," King said. "Those narrow streets with all those trees, and those policemen, scared themselves, calling up into that tree for that man to come down. Thousands of policemen as scared as we were, and anything might come from anywhere."

The phone rang.

Stanley Levison, who was closest to it, picked up the receiver. He identified himself, listened for a moment, then handed the phone to Andy Young, who began a conversation and then suddenly interrupted it. "I'm going to take this in the kitchen," Young said to the others, putting down the receiver. He left the dining room.

In the kitchen, he resumed the conversation. "All right, I can talk now."

The caller was the Reverend Williamson. "Have you spoken to Martin?" he asked.

"No," Young said, "I haven't talked to him. It's impossible."

"He told us he'd come back."

Young said firmly, "He can't say no. I think it's wrong for you to press him. We gave you one march in Memphis, and it almost killed us."

"Andy, nonviolence is on trial now," Williamson said.

"We'll have to vindicate it somewhere else. It's just not—"

Young was interrupted as King's voice came on the line. "This is Martin. When is the march?"

Delighted, Williamson told him, "Friday."

"I'll be there," King promised.

In the kitchen Andy Young slammed the phone

back in its cradle, then strode back to the dining room.

"We're thinking about changing the whole country," he told King. "You can't go back to Memphis. It's an unnecessary risk."

"Williamson is right," King replied. "Nonviolence *is* on trial in Memphis. Besides, they're expecting me. I can't let them down, Andy."

Young sank into a chair, conceding defeat. "I'm frightened for you," he told King.

"I'm frightened, too," King replied. He was silent for a second. "You never get over being frightened," he said. "You think you do, but it's always there around some corner waiting for you, waiting to engulf you, and you have no control over it." He looked around the table at his friends, smiling at them fondly. "But all we ever had to fight with— all any of us ever had to fight with—was to say 'I'm not afraid. Do what you want with us. We're going on.' Once we said that, there was no weapon that could stop us." He looked away again, off into some far distance. "We can't be afraid now."

That evening the King family went to Funtown. "You see, Marty," Coretta said to her son. "I told you you'd get to Funtown. Now, what rides do you want to go on?"

Marty looked around anxiously. "I haven't made up my mind yet." When they passed the revolving airplanes, he smiled. "I want to go on this one."

King went over to buy tickets.

"Martin, what are you doing?" asked Coretta. "You know you can't ride on these things without getting sick."

"He wants to ride it," said King, wanting to do anything to please his son. "What about you?"

Coretta laughed. "Not me."

"Yoki?" King asked.

"I get sick just looking at it," said Yoki.

"Let's go, Marty." King said. He sat with the boy on the revolving airplane.

Marty enjoyed every minute of the ride. Looking at him, King felt guilt for having deprived the child of his presence so many times, and for the possibility that he might not live to be the father that Marty would need to get him into manhood.

He drew his son closer to him, so close that Marty looked up and asked, "Dad, what's the matter?"

At the airport, waiting with Andy, Abernathy, Bernard and the others for the plane that would take them to Memphis, King heard a voice call out.

"Hey! Wait! Wait!"

A.D. came running toward them. "I almost missed you," he said breathlessly.

King was puzzled. "What are you doing?"

"I want to come with you," said A.D.

King looked at him, moved that his kid brother wanted to join him in this moment of trouble.

"All right," he said, putting a hand on A.D.'s shoulder. "Come on."

29

As King and the others drove through Memphis on the way from the airport to the Lorraine Motel, the streets resembled an armed camp. There were policemen on every corner. There were troops. There were garbage workers with signs reading, "I Am A Man."

Andy Young began to have more and more misgivings about being in Memphis. But there was something in the back of his mind that he wanted clarified. "Jerry," he told the Reverend Williamson, "I want to speak to those boys who pushed Martin."

Williamson had managed to identify two of the young men who had attacked King, and he arranged for them to be brought to the Lorraine Motel. Andy wanted to question them one at a time, and as he questioned the first one, whose name was George, King, Bernard and Williamson wondered precisely what he was getting at.

After a while it became clear. Andrew Young did not believe in the conventional militancy that was given as an excuse for disrupting the first Memphis march.

"Why is it you were never interested in the strike before?" Andy asked.

George hesitated. "The guys got me interested in it."

"Why did you push Dr. King? Do you like pushing him?"

George looked at King, alarmed and ashamed. It was as though, without the crowd around him, he was frightened to be in the presence of King.

After a moment, George said, "No. At home they think of him as Jesus Christ."

"Is that how you reward him?" asked Andy. "You push him?"

George addressed King directly. "Dr. King, you have to understand—"

"No! He's not going to understand!" Andy shouted. "None of us is going to understand what you and the others were doing there."

There was a moment of silence.

We were paid," said George miserably.

Even though Andy knew that this was probably the case, he was startled to hear it. "You were paid. By whom?"

"I don't know," George said.

"Let's try the other one," Young told Williamson, and George was taken away.

A moment later Williamson returned with the other man. His name was Louis, and he was in his middle twenties and arrogant.

Andy questioned him fiercely, breaking through his facade of militancy.

"Louis," he said. "You're a son of a bitch! Why were you interested in the strike?"

"He's a Morehouse man. He's got an honors degree," Williamson said.

"We've got to do some fighting! Not marching—

fighting!" said Louis looking at the others as though they were Uncle Toms.

"Don't give me that stuff! The only thing you give a damn about is your own precious behind! A college graduate. An honors degree. And you care about garbage workers? Don't make me laugh!"

"What is this?" Louis snarled. "An inquisition?"

"That's right!" Williamson shouted. "George talked."

Louis looked at him incredulously for a moment, then said, "That stupid bastard."

"Who paid you?" insisted Andy, sensing that now he might be on the edge of a truth that had evaded him for weeks, for months—even years.

There were many times that he had been suspicious of the term "black power," of much of the militancy that had been used against King. It had all been too well organized. The black militants had press conferences and television time at the drop of a hat, while the SCLC had had to fight for every inch. It had all congealed for Andy during the Memphis march. The disruption had been too well organized. He knew the people involved. They were not capable of that kind of orchestration.

"Don't tell people around here," said Louis. With a bitter grin, he indicated King. "They think he's Lord God Almighty."

"Who was it?" asked Andy.

There was a long pause before Louis spoke. The silence filled the room.

"The FBI."

Williamson felt fright. My God, if it was the FBI, what would happen next?

Andy stared at Louis. He had heard what something deep within him had expected to hear—an answer to the questions of the last years. It was brilliant of them. They had taken the white man's fears and capitalized upon them, using young black men in their pay. They had shouted "Black Power!" every moment they could, knowing that the very phrase was incendiary and would turn off the white man. How sad. They had usurped King and the Movement with their own people. But Andy knew that was not new, knew that it was the history of every revolutionary movement from the beginning of time. Those movements that had been broken had been broken from within.

King tried to grapple with the fear inside him. If a government agency would go this far, there might not be any length to which it would not go. (There was a phrase later on in the Church report that said, "King must be neutralized." "Neutralized" was the term used in World War II for destroying a foreign agent.)

"Get him out of here," Andy said at last, nodding at Louis.

William took Louis by the arm to lead him out.

"They had them in a lot of demonstrations," Louis said. "I'm not the only one."

"Get him out!" Andy snapped.

The men sat silent after Louis was gone. They knew now what they were contending with.

"Maybe we should get out of Memphis," said Andy.

King looked at him. "What for?" he said. "Do you think things are going to be different anywhere else?"

Detective Ed Redditt was one of the finest detectives in Memphis. That he had risen so far, that he was held in such trust and esteem by the police department, even though he was a black man, was evidence of his abilities. Redditt was known as his own man; he was the kind of man who was thought to be a born detective. The life appealed to him, the variety of it, the not knowing what would come next.

Now Redditt walked to the fire station that overlooked the Lorraine Motel and went inside. He found a position from which he could observe the courtyard of the motel and took out his binoculars. He made sure his view was clear.

Dave Wallace and Harry Burns, two black firemen, wandered over to him. Burns was an independent, bespectacled man in his 30s. Wallace was slim, alert, good-natured, a man who kept himself physically trim by jogging a few miles every morning.

The two firemen wanted to know what Redditt was doing.

"Security," Redditt replied.

Burns was a friend to the cause. "Do you see him?" he asked, edging in beside Redditt and looking out the window.

"I see the balcony outside his room . . . and the windows," Redditt replied.

"Are you expecting something?" Wallace asked.

Redditt shrugged, lowering the glasses.

"What went wrong last time?"

"I don't know," said the detective. "But nothing's going to go wrong this time. I know everybody who travels with King. I know their cars. I know their license numbers. Anything looks wrong, I'll know about it."

"You going to the meeting tonight?"

"Sure," said Redditt. "I want to hear him speak."

"I'm going to march in the demonstration tomorrow," Burns said with some pride.

Redditt glanced at him sideways. "You could lose your job."

"I don't care," Burns returned. "I know what they're fighting for. I know they're right."

"Dave, Harry . . ." Redditt said, "you two and I are the only black men around here tonight. We're the only ones who give a damn about him. Let me know if you hear anything or see anything, will you?"

Burns and Wallace nodded solemnly.

Redditt raised the glasses again, focusing on the glow from the windows of the suite where the leaders of the march had established their headquarters. A rain was beginning to fall, obscuring his view.

In the bedroom of the motel suite, King sat on the edge of the bed. He had just placed a long distance call to Atlanta. As he waited, he stared distractedly at the windows, scarcely aware of the hard rain beating against the glass. Coretta came on the line.

"Hello, Martin," she said affectionately.

"Did you get your flowers?" he asked.

"Flowers? No."

"I was downtown picking up a suit—"

Coretta broke in, amused. "Don't tell me you broke down and bought a suit!"

"There was a florist next door, and I got you some

flowers," he went on. "The proprietor promised to deliver them right away."

"No," Coretta said. "They— Wait, there's the doorbell. Maybe that's them now."

King waited. In a moment she came back on the line.

"I got them! Red carnations!"

"Good!" he said, pleased.

"Martin, they're beautiful." She hesitated. "But . . . they're artificial. I thought you didn't like artificial flowers."

King smiled. "I wanted to give you something that would last."

Coretta was startled. She wondered if he realized what he had said.

King had just hung up the phone when it rang. It was Ralph Abernathy calling.

"We're meeting here at the church. Listen, you better get over here, Martin."

"What for?"

"They want you."

"I'm tired," King said. "I told you I wasn't going to speak tonight."

"If you don't come over here, they'll come over and get you," warned Abernathy.

King looked at the rain-washed windows. "You're kidding," he said. "Nobody's there in this weather."

Abernathy said, "No? Listen to this."

Over the phone, in the background, King heard shouting and the chanting of his name. He smiled wearily. "All right. I'll be right over."

Nobody who was there would ever forget that evening. A storm raged outside, and there were times when it was necessary to close the windows.

The church itself seemed to shake from the storm.

And Ralph Abernathy, who was usually given to short introductions, spoke for forty-five minutes about his association with King, how much it had meant to him, and about the kind of man this Martin was.

There was enormous applause when King rose. Feeling self-conscious after Abernathy's introduction, he said that there were times he thought Ralph must have been talking about somebody else. The audience laughed good-naturedly. King went on.

"You know, several years ago I was in New York City. I was stabbed. The tip of the blade was on the edge of the aorta of my heart. If I had sneezed, I would have died."

His listeners were absolutely silent.

"A letter came from a little girl," King went on. "It said simply, 'Dear Dr. King: I am a ninth grade student at the White Plains High School. While it should not matter, I would like to mention that I'm a white girl. And I'm simply writing you to say that I'm so happy that you didn't sneeze.'"

There was a murmur of laughter.

"I'm happy, too, that I didn't sneeze," King said. "If I had sneezed, I wouldn't have been around here in 1961 when we decided to take a ride for freedom . . . and ended segregation in interstate travel!

"If I had sneezed, I wouldn't have been here in 1963 when the black people in Birmingham, Alabama, desegregated the most powerful industrial city of the South!

"If I had sneezed, I wouldn't have been down in Selma, Alabama, to see the great movement there

. . . which made it possible to make a voting rights bill . . . so that black people could vote and change the history of this country!

"If I had sneezed, I wouldn't have been in Memphis to see a community rally around the sanitation brothers and sisters who are suffering. Because garbage workers are as important as anybody. They have dignity and they have worth!"

There were cries of agreement and support.

King looked about at the faces of his listeners. He was silent for a few moments. Then he seemed to look inward, as if he were re-experiencing the fears and conflicts of his life.

"Now today . . . we have come into Memphis and some things have happened. And there's talk about what might happen to me from some of our sick white brethren. We've got some difficult days ahead. But it doesn't matter with me now. Because I've been to the mountaintop!"

He turned slightly, looking back at his friends who were seated behind him on the platform, Andy Young and Ralph Abernathy and the others. He smiled fondly, then faced forward again.

"I don't mind. Like anybody," he said, "I would like to live a long life. Longevity has its place. But I'm not concerned about that now. I just want to do God's will. And He's allowed me to go up to the mountain!"

The emotion of the moment had gripped the listeners. Many were weeping silently.

"And I've looked over," he told them. "And I've seen the promised land! I may not get there with you, but I want you to know tonight . . . that we as a people will get to the promised land."

271

King turned his eyes to his brother, who was standing near the platform. He looked at A. D. with love.

Then something else happened. He looked his own adversary, fear, in the face and knew that for some reason he was released from it.

"And I am happy tonight!" he roared, returning his attention to the audience. "I'm not worried about anything! I'm not fearing any man!"—and he meant it. "Mine eyes have seen the glory . . . of the coming of the Lord. . . !"

He turned away, and then the crowd exploded in jubilation, crying out his name.

"King! King!"

He started to turn back to acknowledge the ovation. But all at once exhaustion overcame him. He started to fall. Then Andy Young and Ralph Abernathy had hold of him.

30

At his home that night, fireman Dave Wallace received an unexpected call.

The caller was the fire chief, who said, "Tomorrow's your day off, isn't it?"

"That's right."

"We're transferring you to Station Eight on Friday."

Wallace was puzzled. "Eight?"

"That's right," the chief said.

"Okay."

A few minutes later, fireman Harry Burns had a call from the chief.

"You're transferred to Eleven tomorrow."

"Why?" Burns asked.

"Those are the orders."

Perplexed, Burns looked at his watch. "It's eleven-thirty," he said. "I've never been transferred at eleven-thirty before. Is anything the matter?"

"No."

"Then why the transfer? We're short there."

With finality, the chief said, "Word I got from Holloman. Police."

The line went dead. Baffled, Burns put down the receiver.

Standing at a window of the firehouse, binoculars

at his eyes, Detective Redditt scanned the court-yard of the Lorraine Motel. Behind Redditt, a white fireman sat at a small table, playing solitaire.

A white detective, Lieutenant Woods, entered the firehouse. He looked about, then approached Redditt, who recognized him and smiled faintly.

"Holloman wants to see you," Woods announced.

"I'm on security here," Redditt told him.

"He said right away."

Redditt shrugged. He dropped the binoculars into his jacket pocket, and he and Woods walked toward the door.

On the way Redditt spoke to the solitaire-playing fireman. "Where's Harry?" he asked.

The fireman answered without looking up from the cards. "Transferred."

When Redditt reached the police station a short while later, he went straight to the office of Frank Holloman, the chief of police. Holloman was talk-ing with a man Redditt had never seen before.

Frank Holloman was a charming man with an open, easy-going manner that belied the authority he had. For he was not only chief of police but chief of firemen as well.

He had worked for many years for the FBI in J. Edgar Hoover's office, and had only recently come to Memphis, where he was greatly respected.

"What's happening?" Redditt asked.

Chief Holloman indicated the other man. "This gentleman is from the government. There's been a contract made out on your life."

Redditt looked skeptical.

"He just flew in from Washington," the chief continued. "He has information that there's a contract out of St. Louis on you. I've made a reservation at a motel—we'll move you and your family there for safety."

Redditt stared at the chief, trying to understand what was happening. "No," he said.

"Why?" Holloman asked. "It's for your own good."

"No," Redditt said again, alarmed. "No, let them stay at home. And I'll stay on the streets—or, better yet, at the fire station."

The Chief looked at him levelly. "I'm relieving you from your duty," he told him.

"I'm not going to a motel," Redditt said stubbornly. "If they're going to get me, let them get me on the street and let my family be safe."

"All right. Go wherever you want," Holloman said. "But Detectives Woods and Anderson will go with you."

Redditt looked at Detectives Woods and Anderson, who had just entered the office. He turned back to Holloman. What I'm thinking can't really be true, he thought.

"You're a good man, Redditt," said Holloman firmly. "We don't want to lose you."

Redditt waited, wanting to be reassured.

"This is an order," said Holloman in his most pleasant manner.

Redditt followed Woods and Anderson out the door.

Approaching King's suite in the Lorraine Motel, Andy Young saw that the door was ajar. The room seemed to be empty, but Andy thought he heard something, perhaps in the closet, perhaps in the bathroom.

"Martin," he called warily.

There was no answer.

"Martin!" Alarmed now, Andy walked swiftly to the rear of the room.

Suddenly there was a shriek. Andy jumped as King, A.D., and Bernard charged out of the bathroom. They were all over him. King wrestled Andy down to the bed.

"Hey, what the hell's the matter with you?" Andy shouted, laughing.

King began to tickle him.

"You think you can always go off on your own?"

"I was in court about the injunction!" Andy yelled.

"What's the matter? Don't you have a nickel? Did you break your finger?"

Andy laughed again.

"How many times must we tell you—you got to call in, man! You got to let the leader know what's going on!" King was mocking himself, his manner full of self-parody.

Everyone was laughing now, as King went on tickling Andy.

"You know, Andy," King said, "Ralph and I were going to call you in court, pull you right out of that room and call you anything but a child of God."

Now the others began to pummel Andy with pillows, and soon the war was enlarged. Bernard hit King with a pillow. King called to A.D. for aid. Instead, A.D. hit King with a pillow.

"Oh, so you're a turncoat, are you?" King grabbed

A.D. and hurled him down on the bed. "Now I'm gonna knock the black off you!"

A.D. writhed, laughing, on the bed, as the others took his socks off and tickled the bottom of his feet. It was one of the happiest, most memorable moments they had shared together.

Later that afternoon, King stood on the balcony of the Lorraine Motel, dressed and ready to leave for dinner at the home of the Reverend Billy Kyles, a personable, thoughtful minister of whom King was particularly fond.

King called into Ralph Abernathy's room to tell him to hurry. Abernathy had just finished shaving.

From the courtyard below the balcony, Jesse Jackson, a rising young recruit to the SCLC, who was making his imprint on the Movement and who had been enormously helpful in Chicago, called out. "Martin?"

King looked down.

"Doc, this is Ben Branch," Jesse said. "He used to live in Memphis. He plays in our band."

"Oh, yes," King called down. "You're my man. How are you, Ben?"

Ben Branch's greeting drifted up. "Hi, Doc."

"Ben, I want you to play for me tonight," King told him. "I want you to play 'Precious Lord, Take My Hand' on the organ. Play it really pretty."

"I sure will, Doc."

Now the elderly man who always drove for King when he was in Memphis called up to the balcony. "It's getting cool, Dr. King. You better get a coat."

Andy and Bernard were with the others in the courtyard. A sound from somewhere behind them—

it was like a backfire—made Andy turn. When he looked up at the balcony again, he saw King's leg protruding over the edge. It was moving.

"Come on, Martin," he called. "This is no time to be horsing around."

Then he saw that Abernathy and other men were crouching on the balcony or running along it toward King.

Andy, Bernard, and Jesse raced up the motel stairs and out onto the balcony. By now there were shouts and screams from everywhere. King was lying by the door to his room. One side of his face had been shattered.

Bending over King, Bernard noticed a neat bullet hole through his tie. It had seemed strange to him; he had helped King tie the knot earlier that evening. The bullet had entered through the neck and gone through the side of his face.

Everybody was screaming, "Get an ambulance!"

"Martin!" shouted Abernathy. "Martin, can you hear me? Martin!"

"God! God! God! God! God!" moaned A.D.

"Get an ambulance!" Andy demanded.

Someone darted into the bathroom and emerged a moment later with an armload of towels.

Andy held King's wrist. "Do you feel anything?" asked Abernathy. Andy shook his head.

"I can't reach the operator," Bernard cried from inside the room. "I can't reach the operator!!"

"My God!" someone cried. "Get an ambulance!"

Those on the balcony did not learn till later that the woman on the floor below King had seen him shot and been felled by a heart attack.

"Call an ambulance!" Andy shouted again.

The voice of a policeman, who had appeared suddenly, inexplicably, in the courtyard below, rose to the balcony. "It's on the way!"

There was the shriek of a siren.

Policemen were setting up a barrier, keeping the curious from crowding into the courtyard.

The ambulance arrived. Paramedics, carrying a stretcher, came hurrying up to the room.

"Careful . . . careful . . ." Andy Young urged as King was placed on the stretcher.

King was borne away, through the room, down the stairs, across the courtyard, with his friends following.

"Can we go with you?" Abernathy asked one of the paramedics as King was being placed in the ambulance.

"Room for one," the paramedic said.

Andy Young touched Abernathy's arm. "You go, Ralph," he said.

In the King home in Atlanta, Coretta and Yolanda were in the living room, watching television. The three other children were upstairs. When the phone rang, Coretta answered it.

"Hello . . ."

Andy Young said gently, "Coretta . . . Doc's been shot. Why don't you take the next plane here? Bring someone with you. We're at St. Joseph's Hospital."

Coretta could hardly speak. "Is it bad?"

There was a long silence before Young said simply, "He's not dead."

Yolanda, her attention drawn to the sudden

change in her mother's tone, glanced toward her. "What is it?" she asked.

At that same instant, the television program was interrupted for a news bulletin, and out of the corner of her eye, Yolanda saw her father's face flash on the screen.

A voice began to speak of an event that had become all too familiar in American life—a prominent figure had been struck down. "This evening at 6:15, Martin Luther King . . ."

Yolanda leaped up. "Don't tell me!" she shrieked, running from the room. "Don't tell me!"

Coretta hung up the phone. "I'm going to Memphis," she said.

At St. Joseph's Hospital in Memphis, Ralph Abernathy, Bernard Lee, and Andy Young stood inside the entrance of the operating room. Their expressions were a mixture of anxiety and desperate hope as they watched and waited. All that King's friends could see of him were brief glimpses of the undamaged portion of his face; the only sound was the head surgeon's crisp orders to the assistants and nurses.

One of the nurses, suddenly becoming aware of Young, Lee, and Abernathy, left the table and moved to where they were standing.

"You can't stay here!" she whispered sharply. "You have to leave."

"Your business is there," Bernard answered, nodding toward the table. "Don't worry about us. We're not going to leave."

She turned and went back.

The flurries of activity at the table increased

Young's, Lee's and Abernathy's anxiety. There were moments, when the head surgeon spoke easily and casually, that raised their hope. Then the surgeon straightened and left the table. Unfastening his mask, he walked to where King's friends were standing.

"I'm sorry," he said. "We've lost him."

The cleaning up at the operating table was already beginning.

Ralph Abernathy walked quietly out, leaving a large portion of his life in that room.

Andy Young was more visibly affected. Andy had enormous emotions, an ocean of them, but he had always kept them down because he knew he must appear cool if he was to be effective. But at this moment, there was no reason to be effective. The tears clouded his eyes, then ran like streams. He left the operating room.

Bernard Lee remained. Lying before him was a man he had known since Montgomery. King had been father, brother, friend—and in a way, son—to him.

Bernard approached the table.

King's face showed the enormous exhaustion he had felt during these last weeks. One of the nurses turned his head and pressed a towel over his wound.

Bernard moved closer and stared at the face on the table. He had to take just one last look.

Detective Redditt's mother-in-law heard the news on the radio, even though they had tried to keep it from her because of her heart condition. When she heard, she had a relapse.

There were many people stricken that day, so close did so many feel to King. Redditt's mother-in-law had cried out, "Dr. King! Dr. King! Why couldn't God have taken me instead of Dr. King?"

Redditt paced the rooms of his house, feeling guilty, feeling responsible. King had been murdered only minutes after Redditt had been transferred from the fire station. He had heard the news on his car radio even before he reached home.

Redditt's thoughts raced.

"They transferred Wallace, Burns and me . . . three black men who cared about King. Things like that don't happen by accident. They just don't happen that way! They'll never make me believe it was coincidental! Never! They killed him! I should have stayed there no matter what! I should have stayed!"

At the Atlanta airport, Coretta hurried to make the plane to Memphis. She held the ticket in her hand. She felt the ticket was her passport to Martin. As long as she held onto that ticket, he would be alive.

The voice over the loud speaker called, "Mrs. Martin Luther King! Mrs. Martin Luther King!"

Coretta stopped. The mayor of Atlanta, Ivan Allen, Jr., his wife, and some aides came up to her. With them was Dora, King's secretary.

Mayor Allen said, "Mrs. King, perhaps if we could go some place . . ."

"Tell me," said Coretta.

Mayor Allen, bearly able to get the words out, said, "Dr. King is dead."

Coretta looked at him, then down at the ticket.

Many things went through her mind at that moment. There was the tremendous shock of knowing she would spend the rest of her life without the man she loved. And there was something else. The grandeur of his life passed through her mind, and the sureness of his knowledge of the sacrifice he would eventually make.

At the door of Martin Luther King Sr.'s house, Chief Jenkins, Chief of Police of Atlanta, an old family friend, stood before King senior. There were tears in the Chief's eyes. He could hear Martin's mother crying inside the house. She knew that her son was hurt, but not yet that he was killed.

"It is my sad duty to tell you your son is dead," said Chief Jenkins. "He died at eight-thirty."

King senior stared at him for a moment. Then he said, "He always told me it would come, but my greatest wish was that I would go before him."

In Stanley Levison's house, he and his wife sat watching the endless television reviews of King's life, and listening to the conversation that said so little about what that life really was and what it really meant.

Stanley spoke at last. "They had to kill him. He was too important."

Back at the Lorraine Motel, A.D. sat alone in his room. He had been told the news, but he had known before he was told. It was hours before he emerged from the room.

The others looked at him. He went by them. They asked where he was going.

"Where are the reporters?" A.D. asked. "Where are the reporters?"

"What's the matter, A.D.?" asked McKeecham.

"I want to talk to them!" A.D. said. "I want to tell them how I feel about the way they killed my brother! I want to tell them how they killed somebody who only loved people, who only wanted to do well for them! I want to tell them what white America did to him!"

He walked toward the reporters who, like so many scavengers, were eager to pick up any bits of information they could.

The others stopped A.D., held him from going forward. Tears streamed from his eyes. "Did you see the way he looked?" he asked. "Did you see the way he looked? Who did it to <u>him</u>? I want to speak to them!"

"You don't want to do that," they said. "He wouldn't have wanted you to."

"Does Daddy know?" asked A.D. "Where's Daddy?" He went on desperately. "He liked people. He always tried to look out for them."

A.D. looked at the others, seeking reassurance, a reassurance that they all sought, that Martin Luther King had really lived. They wanted him alive as long as they could, even though he was dead.

"Where is he?" shouted A.D. "Where's my brother?"

Dr. Franciscus, Medical Examiner of Memphis, was beginning to perform the autopsy on King.

Abernathy had made the formal identification. Andy remained now to see no autopsy notes were destroyed, as they had been in Dallas after John Kennedy's autopsy.

A.D. came into the autopsy room. He screamed when he saw the remains of Martin on the table.

"It isn't all of him," said Andy quietly. "It isn't all of him."

And it wasn't all of him.

The speech in the Montgomery church about the bus boycott, the willingness to sacrifice himself again and again—in Montgomery, in Birmingham, in Selma, in Chicago, in Memphis—all this was still in the hearts of the sanitation workers who stood outside St. Joseph's Hospital in Memphis carrying signs that read: "I Am A Man."

And all this was in the hearts of the people who followed a home-made cart drawn by a donkey as it carried the remains of Martin Luther King to his final resting place.

There were presidents, ex-presidents, and other celebrated people from all over the world. But few of them were the equal of Martin Luther King, because King, unlike almost all other men in public life, had been willing to put first the things he believed, and himself second.

And King was alive, too, in Yolanda as she watched the sea of people that surrounded the donkey and the cart. She thought: "Andy Young said to me that one day there will be black mayors and black Congressmen, and even black presidents will be elected because of what Daddy did." But to Yolanda, King was a real man, her father; she remembered how he used to come home and say, "Where's my sugar? Can't we freeze Yoki just as she is?"

He had left her this: She would never be able to hate anybody. And she knew that he had marked everybody who had known him.

"So maybe he's not gone," she thought. "Maybe he's more alive than anyone I know."

And all those who had known him, even for an instant—they had been to the mountaintop too.

THE BEST OF THE BESTSELLERS
FROM WARNER BOOKS!

BLUE SKIES, NO CANDY by Gael Greene   (81-368, $2.50)
"How in the world were they able to print **Blue Skies, No Candy** without some special paper that resists Fahrenheit 451? (That's the burning point of paper!) This sizzling sexual odyssey elevates Ms. Greene from her place at the head of the food-writing list into the Erica Jong pantheon of sexually liberated fictionalists."—**Liz Smith, New York Daily News**

THESE GOLDEN PLEASURES   (82-416, $2.25)
by Valerie Sherwood
From the stately mansions of the east to the freezing hell of the Klondike, beautiful Roxanne Rossiter went after what she wanted —and got it all! By the author of the phenomenally successful THIS LOVING TORMENT.

THIS LOVING TORMENT   (82-649, $2.25)
by Valerie Sherwood
Perhaps she was too beautiful! Perhaps the brawling colonies would have been safer for a plainer girl, one more demure and less accomplished in language and manner. But Charity Woodstock was gloriously beautiful with pale gold hair and topaz eyes —and she was headed for trouble.

BLOOD OF THE BONDMASTER   (82-385, $2.25)
by Richard Tresillian
Bolder and bigger than **The Bondmaster, Blood of the Bondmaster** continues the tempestuous epic of Roxborough plantation, where slaves are the prime crop and the harvest is passion and rage.

Ⓦ A Warner Communications Company

THE BEST OF THE BESTSELLERS
FROM WARNER BOOKS!

I, CLEOPATRA by William Bostock   **(81-379, $2.50)**
A big ancient-historical romance about history's first and foremost femme fatale. **I, Cleopatra** presents a striking new interpretation of the most famous sextress of all time: her own story as told by herself.

PASSION AND PROUD HEARTS   **(82-548, $2.25)**
by Lydia Lancaster
The sweeping saga of three generations of a family born of a great love and torn by the hatred between North and South. The Beddoes family——three generations of Americans joined and divided by love and hate, principle and promise.

HOWARD HUGHES: THE HIDDEN YEARS   **(89-521, $1.95)**
by James Phelan
The book of the year about the mystery man of the century——a startling eyewitness account by two of the aides who were closest to Hughes in his last secret years. "A compelling portrait . . . the best picture that we are likely to see."——**The New York Times Book Review**

MOSHE DAYAN: STORY OF MY LIFE AN AUTOBIOGRAPHY
by Moshe Dayan   **(83-425, $2.95)**
"A first-rate autobiography by a man who has been at the center of Israel's political and military life since before the rise of the state."——**Heritage.** 16 pages of photographs.

 A Warner Communications Company